Eden's Veil

by Steve Kern

Kern Enterprises
OKLAHOMA CITY

Also by Steve Kern:

Eden's Son
Eden's Tears
No Other Gods

Eden's Veil

Cover design by Phyllis Mantik

ISBN 978-0-9634981-3-7

This book is dedicated to all those who, like Baqash, are honest seekers of the truth in a dark and deadly world. May you find the truth in Jesus Christ, the ultimate "seed of the woman."

Table of Contents

Foreword

The world and all its creation are obviously quite special in the period between the fall of man and the Great Flood. This time of earth's history (approximately 1500 years) is veiled in the brevity of three chapters of Genesis (chapters 3-6), and virtually all we know about this time is found in those verses.

We are confident that the curse was so inclusive that all of creation (man, woman, animals, and the earth) was genetically manipulated as a result. However, it doesn't seem the effects were immediate; rather, they developed in intensity as the flood period approached.

Using a fictional genre, Steve Kern makes an interesting attempt at illustrating the uniqueness of this era. In flights of descriptive fancy, he paints breath-catching scenes of both the environment and spiritual relationships that may have existed during this obscure time.

You will find that reading this story is exciting and enlightening, for most of the extensions of this remarkable narrative are, we believe, true to the predictions you would make about the pre-flood age.

The fact that God created all land-dwelling animals on day six of the creation week tells us that the giant reptiles would have existed with man. Furthermore, all animals, plants, and man would have lived much longer during this time in earth's history due to the special effects of day two of the creation week. In addition, many of earth's climatic manifestations that began at creation continued in the same pristine manner, providing environmental uniqueness right up to the time of Noah's flood.

All these factors are carefully woven into the plot, personalities, and passion of this most intriguing novel. You will find it hard to put down once you begin reading.

G. Thomas Sharp, Ph.D.
April 2000

Preface

It is important to read the introduction before beginning to read this book. The story takes place in the pre-flood world, which was very different from the earth we now know. This introduction gives a description of that world along with some of the scientific implications the different environment would have produced. Further, to have a greater appreciation of the earth's pre-flood environment, it is useful to refer to Genesis 1-6. *Eden's Veil* was written to help the reader develop a mental picture of the pre-flood world in these chapters while attempting to provide a story that is entertaining and inspiration. Remember, this is a book of fiction in a biblical context that provides a means to communicated important spiritual truths that apply to all generations.

Introduction

The Earth That Was

It was a time long since forgotten, in a place no longer known. The earth was a world of great contrast, full of lush beauty overshadowed by the violence of an unprincipled human population. Humankind no longer knew the benevolent God who had created them, and all but a few had given their hearts and minds to follow the worship of the sinister serpent god, Lucifer. Those were days of creation's bright glory, unseen by dark hearts.

This is the story of a man named Baqash, "one who seeks." He is representative of many men in each generation who have tried to find truth in the midst of contradictions such as good and evil, love and hate, beauty and ugliness, joy and pain, and life and death. These conflicts lead to pressing questions of life. Baqash seeks to answer these questions: What does it all mean? Is there any sense that can be made of it all? Were these riddles the original intention of the Creator? Is there a Creator at all? If there is a Creator, which god is the right one? The dilemmas of life have always raised many questions to which the honest of heart must find the answers. Baqash searches to find the truth about these contradictions in his world.

Baqash lived in the days before the global flood described in the Bible. It was a world much different from what it is now, except for one common characteristic: the heart of every man in each generation still has a void that can only be filled by the God who made us in His image. This God works hard to fill that void in those who seek Him with a whole heart.

What glorious beauty there was in the earth in those days! It was enclosed by a crystal-clear, protective water vapor covering, eleven miles in the sky. This shield of crystalline, vaporized water acted as a wonderful, transparent enhancer of the lights in the heavens and provided a perfect environment for the growth of all kinds of life on land and in the seas.

As the sun shone clearly through the vapor shield during the day, the crystalline shield was warmed evenly as it encircled the earth from pole to pole. As a result, the temperatures over the surface of the whole earth remained fairly uniform year-round, ranging from as high as 78 degrees to a low of 72 degrees.

The night was a dazzling sight as the water canopy acted like a magnifying glass to brighten the stars and the moon, causing each to be seen in smashing brilliance against the backdrop of black velvet space. The stars could be seen so clearly that each could be read like a book that tells the time and the seasons.

There was never a cloud in the sky to hide the brightness of the sun or to cover the stars at night. Streams and the water within the earth rose in a gentle mist in the early morning and fell like dew to the ground, providing moisture to plant life for abundant growth. There were no stormy winds to rage or torrent rains to fall, for the constant worldwide temperatures, low-lying, rolling hills, and gently rising mountains gave no cause for such disruption to the intended tranquility. The only disruption came from the human element as people ravaged one another in the calm.

The benevolent, spherical protective tent in which the Creator had placed His earth acted like a guard at the gate of a city. It allowed all the long, life-giving light waves to pass through but turned away the destructive short waves. This guard at the gate turned away those forces that might cause mutation and disease. It also caused the atmospheric pressure to be twice what is now known. This increase in pressure had wonderful effects on the healing processes of the body. The absence of disease and heightened healing capacity made it possible for humans and animals to live for very long periods of time. Those who died young did so violently, for there were no enemies of health except very old age and man's tools of war and murder.

The increase in atmospheric pressure provided far more oxygen in the air due to the much greater amount of plant life that covered the whole earth with thick tropical forests blended with square miles of plains covered with lush green grasses. The struggle for human survival was not due to droughts, floods, hail storms, or insects but to thorns and thistles that had to be continually turned back from taking over what was grown for food. This was important, for in those days man ate only that which came out of the ground.

The thorns and thistles were a puzzle to those who worked the ground to provide food for their cities and towns. They were like a curse in what could have been a perfect world. Those who had to fight the weeds paid a heavy price in sweat for the struggle it took to keep them controlled, and they shed blood from the thorns that pricked and cut at will. It was a mystery to them how the weeds grew so much more quickly than other plants. It seemed they had a mandate to overrun the earth and make man's life miserable.

The priests of the serpent god, Lucifer, told the people that the weeds were his gift to man. The sweat that the weeds placed on man's brow and the blood the thorns brought forth from his hands were the sacrifice that made his food offerings acceptable and pleasing to Lucifer. Their book of worship told them, "Without the sweat of the brow and the blood of man's hands, Lucifer will not be appeased."

The increase in atmospheric pressure and the heavy concentration of oxygen in the air and water made it possible for man and animals, plant life and insects, to grow very large. Long lives also made it possible for many animals that grew all their lives to grow into massive giants. These very large animals were necessary to this tropical ecosystem, which needed to be continually grazed by animals that could consume foliage by the tons. What magnificent and powerful specimens these huge beasts were! They often could be used to man's advantage as he learned the secrets of bringing them under his control.

All animals of that time were herbivores, and some were scavengers that fed on what had died, but none had become hunters or true carnivores until man taught them how. They were peaceful grazers unless frightened or provoked. But there was one beast of all beasts, one that was easily provoked and aroused fear in all living things. These leviathans lived as individual hermits in the depths of the seas, but they would attack any who dared to invade their exclusive domains. Many were the bones on the sea floor of those who had foolishly tried. Each of these beasts was larger than any other creature, and each had the ability to breathe fire and smoke. Their large, thick-as-iron scales were so closely meshed together that it was virtually impossible to kill one with lance, spear, or arrow. The roar of this monster could fill the heavens and the earth with dread. Man had charted the seas to avoid the domains of these fierce ones.

There were times when this beast left its natural marine habitat to cross land in search of less inhabited waters. Leviathan would do this to establish its new domain when defeated in battle by a stronger adversary. At these times, leviathan was even more dangerous for it was not in its natural environment. It felt threatened by any living or non-living object that found itself in the monster's way.

Earth was completely populated in those days, and there were no continents separated by vast oceans. Man and all living creatures were free to migrate all over the globe. The constant temperatures took away the need for adaptation, for the environment was the same everywhere. The oceans were more like huge lakes that dotted the large areas of land. The lands were not separated by vast, imposing mountain ranges but were interconnected by vast flat lands, interspersed with mild rolling hills and low mountains covered in tropical beauty. All was covered with wonderful trees, bushes, grasses, and flowers. Only greed and constant warring among the different human tribes and nations caused separation.

Safety was a luxury that belonged only to the strong and the crafty.

Earth's human population had spread around the earth, and people lived in large cities and towns. They shared a common language that allowed individuals to communicate freely anywhere in the world. These humans were very intelligent, and they lived in sculptured, open-air houses that were built with walls to provide privacy and protection from thieves while allowing them to see the sky by night and day. There was no need to protect themselves from the forces of nature because there was nothing from which they needed protection. They had developed crystalline receivers from the rocks and sand that captured music from the stars. They also made their own instruments and made music of much variety. They listened most to that which stirred their deepest, lustful desires.

Mankind had also learned the secrets of working with metal and could produce many metals not possible to develop in the changed environment after the flood. They accumulated much gold and silver and all the many kinds of precious stones. Those who had learned to control their fellow men accumulated possessions unto themselves, and many of their home furnishings and fine woven linen clothes were laced with exquisite gold and silver designs, accented by all manner of precious jewels.

Many who lived in the cities were slaves to those stronger than they were. They were members of tribes who had been subdued in the constant battles for supremacy of the provincial warlords. They worked in the homes and fields of those who had gained control of them by force and sedition. Those who were the most fit and adaptable were those who survived.

Cities and provinces that became the most powerful were those that could woo one of the great men of renown to be their champion protector. These huge humanoid giants were the product of the sexual union of fallen angels, called "sons of God," and the daughters of the human race. These fallen angels, as followers of Lucifer, could transform themselves and take on human-like bodies; then, for a season, they took human women as their wives.

The male offspring of these unions grew to be head and shoulders taller than any human. The tallest of men, who were an average of seven to nine feet tall, could only reach the waist or lower chest of one of these giants, who ranged from fourteen to sixteen feet tall. These giants were fierce fighters among themselves and against humans and animals. Thus they became known as "the Violent Ones." They were self-centered tyrants who always had to be appeased with wine, music, women, and wealth They were intelligent and received demonic power from their fallen angelic parents. They brought much grief to the humans they lived among, yet these humans had learned to use them to their advantage much of the time.

The mothers of these freaks of fallen creation were sacrificed to Lucifer soon after they were born, for the babies were holy to the serpent god. The mothers were holy as well. The baby boys were raised by the priests of Lucifer in hidden monasteries around the globe. They were schooled in all the dark things of Lucifer. If daughters were born by these unnatural unions, they were sacrificed to Lucifer as most holy offerings. The mothers of the girl babies, like the mothers of the boy babies, were also sacrificed lest they be defiled by any further union with demon or man. Their blood was poured on the head of the serpent idol in the main temple at Hellsrun. As the priest poured out this blood, he spoke mysterious words: "Thy seed shall not bruise me."

Hellsrun was the holy city of the world. Other cities had temples, but they all existed in submission to Hellsrun. This town was a huge metropolis with a population of millions that spread over the northern center point of the earth. At the very center of Hellsrun stood the multi-tiered, megalithic Temple of the Serpent, which reached forty stories into the sky. The pinnacle of this temple stood directly beneath the North Star, the center and controller of all other stars and stellar formations.

Each year millions of pilgrims made journeys to the temple to have the temple priests bless them and tell them their future written in the stars. They also joined in the worship of Lucifer as they witnessed the sacrifices of the holy women and holy female babies. A trip to Hellsrun, also known as the Holy Rite of Passage, was something every male human had to make at least once before the end of his fiftieth year. These men made the trip to receive the mark of Lucifer on their hands or foreheads. Women received the mark in a local temple when they came of marriageable age. The mark allowed an individual to receive total acceptance in all areas of society. Not having the mark meant disgrace and made it almost impossible to survive. The earlier in life a man made the trip, the more blessed would be the rest of his life. Those who failed to make this trip were tracked down and killed or enslaved as enemies of Lucifer.

This was the kind of world in which Baqash lived—a world of great beauty and even greater depravity. It was in this world that Baqash would make his search for the truth about his own existence, and it was in this world that Baqash would attempt the quest that many make in their own generation: the search for Eden.

One

Arrangement in Madigan

I intend for Baqash to rule this city in a few revolutions of earth around the sun—and my whole domain after I have been absorbed back into Lucifer, Lemish!"

"Ha, should he live so long, Cainogan! You have named him well, for a seeker he is, and his questions will bring the wrath of Lucifer down on us all. Men do not live long who question the holy writings and the Serpent's ways. You would have done your son a service had you forced him to forget his questions and learn to accept things as they are. I will not trade my daughter, Landua, to you unless Baqash makes his journey to Hellsrun by the end of this revolution around the sun. I will not give my daughter in marriage to a man cursed of the serpent. When he returns from Hellsrun, I will consider your offer." Lemish left Cainogan with his thoughts as he hurried out of the palace of Madigan, the capital of the Cainogan province.

Lemish is right, thought Cainogan, the great warrior king of one of the larger provinces of the earth. *It is wrong for Baqash to expect Lemish to trade his daughter to us as long as he continues to put off his journey to Hellsrun. Why can't he be like the other young men and accept the teachings of the serpent priests? I get so angry with him and his foolish rebellion! If he were not such a great warrior and hero of the people, I would give one of my other sons the position at my right hand. I will tell him tomorrow when he comes that if he wants Landua to wed, he will have to lay aside his foolish rebellion and do what is expected of us all.*

Baqash was expected to give his report to his father the next day concerning his battles with the province to the east of their own. The Damogan people were continually trying to enlarge their borders at the expense of the Cainogans. Baqash was the youngest of Cainogan's many sons, but he had proven himself an able leader at a very young age. He was strong and handsome and showed much cunning in war. He was also someone Cainogan felt he could trust. Cainogan had lived several hundred revolutions around the sun and knew that there were those in his own family who would rise up against him if they felt they had a chance to establish their own domain. With all his frustration with Baqash, Cainogan loved this child of his old age, and he knew Baqash loved him.

"Baqash is ready to meet with your magnificence," said the keeper of the door to Cainogan's private state room.

"I receive him," replied Cainogan, his anticipation mixed with frustration.

Baqash entered the room hurriedly, bowed respectfully before his father, and then stood and faced the older man, wanting to embrace him as he had done as a child. But that would show weakness, something no warrior had a right to display. "Father, it is an honor to be in your presence again," he said warmly and sincerely.

"I, too, am glad to see you, my son," replied Cainogan. "Have a seat, and tell me how your encounter with the Damogans fared."

"Well, Father, we were able to subdue them again, but it seems they get stronger each time we battle. They are developing better weapons than they have had before, and I hear they are trying to lure one of the Violent Ones away from Hellsrun to replace the champion they have now. If they can do that, our own warriors will lose heart, for our Violent One will be no match for one who has been chosen to protect Hellsrun. Besides, Father, I believe our champion is losing his commitment to us. He keeps asking for more gold and food and wine and women. He could turn on us, Father."

"Yes, I have had my own concerns about Boax. We may have to do away with him before he does away with us," replied Cainogan to his son, his concern evident.

"Father," Baqash replied, a hint of nervousness in his voice. "I don't want to sound like I'm not aware that this is a grave situation, but I have been very anxious to hear what Lemish said in reply to our offer to trade for Landua."

Cainogan felt himself get angry with his son for making the matter of a woman more important than matters of war. But as his face turned an explosive red, the look on his son's face reminded him of how much he had loved Baqash's mother many revolutions before. "Son," he said, his temper cooling a bit. "Lemish has a strong point to which I agree. He will not trade Landua unless you are willing to make the trip to Hellsrun within this passing around the sun. We do not need the wrath of Lucifer on our house or the house of Lemish."

"But Father, you know how I feel about all that," countered Baqash, his own anger rising. "I question a god who can make a creation such as the one we live in, which is so full of beauty and wonder, and yet be so full of violence and bloodshed. Father, how could a god like Lucifer, who slaughters beautiful women for sacrifice, put the love in my heart that I feel for Landua? I can't bring myself to give my allegiance to a god who causes us to live under the tyranny that Lucifer has brought on us all. If Lucifer is god, then I curse the day he made me!"

Cainogan slapped his son with all the force he had in his body. "How can you speak such blasphemy in the presence of your father? I have allowed you much freedom of thought, but I never thought you would show this kind of rebellion to my face."

Blood seeped from the side of Baqash's mouth, and with tears in his eyes he cried, "Yes! And now see what Lucifer has done to us! A father slaps his son in the name of Lucifer. All hail, mighty Lucifer! Hail to the one who shines!"

Cainogan was cut to the quick, but in order to not show any sign of weakness, he stood his ground before his brokenhearted son. In his heart he felt great respect for this youth who was willing to openly say what he had many times felt in his own heart but pushed aside as foolishness. He had lost a beautiful daughter to motherhood of a Violent One and sacrifice to Lucifer. It was supposed to be a great honor, but something inside him never allowed him to accept the honor. Instead it gave him pain—pain he hid because it was wrong or even dangerous to question the serpent god.

Baqash collected himself and then said quietly to his somber father, "I will go to Hellsrun if that is what it will take for me to have

Landua as my wife. I may bow my knee to Lucifer, but I will never bow my heart. It will also be well for me to go there to try to win away the Violent One from the Damogans. But I must say this is a bad time for me to be gone so long, Father. There could be another assault. We pushed back the Damogans for a time, but their will was not completely broken."

Cainogan was silent in response to his son's offer. He understood that Baqash was bowing to his will, and he did not want to shame his son with condescending words of empty authority. Instead he did something he had not done since Baqash was a small boy. He embraced his son with deep admiration and whispered, "Go, my son, and may your arm of strength sustain you."

The palace of Madigan was a beautiful and spacious place with high walls that rose five stories in tiered sections, allowing the outward tiers to be open to the soft pink daytime sky and the luminous, star-filled skies of the night. The very top floor of the palace was completely open to the glorious view, and Baqash remembered how as a small boy he had lain awake at night, counting the stars and learning all their formations, which suggested where the earth was in orbit around the sun. He counted the orbits as he looked forward to the day he could become a warrior prince and take Landua, the girl he had been attracted to since childhood, to be his first and foremost wife. Men who could afford to trade for wives had as many as they could afford—that is, those women who were not taken by the Sons of God.

Baqash left the palace behind as he rode toward Lemish's mansion on his splendid, two-legged megalosaur war lizard. Megalosaurs were perfectly suited animals for battle with tremendous speed, mobility, and no sense of fear when rightly trained. The mansion was a few streets down from the palace toward the center of the city where the temple stood. Landua lived not far from the temple.

Baqash had made arrangements with Lemish to meet with Landua before he began the long journey to Hellsrun. It was a dangerous thing to meet with a woman once she began to come of age. She was worth much gold and silver to her family as long as she remained undefiled. A father had the right to take the life of any man who defiled his daughter before he could trade her. Of course a Son of God would take a daughter as a gift. A father did not desire his daughters to be too beautiful, for then they were more likely to be traded than given to a Son of God.

Baqash never desired to defile Landua because she had become a friend as much as she was the woman who owned his heart. Nevertheless, Lemish always made sure there were guards there to protect his interests when the two met together. They always met in the courtyard on the ground floor, a space filled with flowers and trees and grass. The trees made it possible for them to steal a kiss or two before a guard could find them. Falenish was an old guard who always turned his head more than the others, and he was on watch this day of parting.

The young couple separated their lips as they heard Falenish give a nervous sigh behind them. "Oh Landua, I would circle the earth a hundred times if that would make it possible for me to finally have you as my own!" Baqash said in words that trembled as

Landua slowly pulled away from his embrace.

"I know you would, Baqash, but it is an evil world we live in, and many of those who journey to Hellsrun never return. I would that you could stay here with me and never leave, but alas, it is the way of our lord, the serpent god."

"He may be your lord, but he will never be mine," spat Baqash, offended.

"Baqash, I wish you would be careful how you talk about the lord Lucifer. I fear he knows all things and nothing escapes his listening ear. You will fall under his judgment, and we will have no future together."

"Landua, I did not arrange this meeting to discuss Lucifer. As far as I know, I may already be under his judgment, but my love for you is far greater than Lucifer himself, and I shall return to claim you as my own, regardless of what comes." The couple stood looking into each other's eyes, trying to absorb as much of this final moment together as they humanly could. Finally Baqash broke the silence. "Please kiss me one final time, and then I must go."

Baqash left Landua at the door of the outer courtyard and mounted his megalosaur. He took one last look and then turned and rode away. It would take at least a full revolution of the earth around the sun to complete his journey to Hellsrun.

Two

The Journey to Hellsrun

Baqash had a long way to travel. The city of Madigan was in the southern hemisphere, eight thousand miles from Hellsrun at the northernmost tip of the earth. Having the luxury of a speedy megalosaur would allow him to travel at a speed of fifty miles per hour. A good, strong animal could run 300 miles without becoming too winded in the dense, highly oxygenated atmosphere. A rider would have to stop more often than that, though, because even the best conditioned riders could not maintain the sustained lunging motion for more than four hours without taking a break. It was fast travel, but it was not the easy travel of wagons and chariots pulled by the larger but slower four-footed horses, rhinoceroses, or triceratops.

It was also not very safe travel. There were renegade tribes who lived off travelers, whom they robbed and often murdered. Each provincial lord used his own soldiers to keep these menaces under control, but they were never fully successful. There were also roaming Violent Ones who had not become champions of cities or provinces or had been run off by others more cunning or stronger than themselves. And then there were dangers when traveling by sea, where there lurked the possibility that a leviathan might have established a new domain that had not yet been charted. The sea barges were often in danger of being capsized by one of these temperamental giants. The human population was going to have to find a way to bring these beasts under control, or they would have to discontinue the use of sea travel.

Baqash was glad his father had given Megado to him as a traveling partner. Megado was a young slave of the Cainogan household who had not yet made his trip to Hellsrun. He had lived all twenty-nine of his revolutions around the sun as a slave, and Baqash, twenty revolutions his senior, had trained him in the ways of war and survival. He was still very young and naïve about many things in life, but he would be a good companion and support in battle if they encountered any trouble.

The two men rode silently along the wide road as they leaned forward in their saddles to take away the wind resistance to their bodies. Their saddles were designed to allow the rider of the megalosaur to lie forward on the animal's back as it gained speed, jutting its head forward and raising its tail in a straight, aerodynamic line behind him.

There were many roads in that day that were important to travel by the provincial warlords' armies for the protection of their boundaries. They were also used by the many travelers to Hellsrun as well as other large cities, but the roads were mostly used by the field workers who brought in the harvest four times per revolution. They needed wide roads that could handle the large wagons drawn by the huge, long-necked dinosaurs, mammoths, and elephants.

As Baqash and Megado traveled, they often had to slow for these wagons.

Travelers had to keep moving through each province on the main roads. They could not bring attention to themselves, or they might be seen as spies or renegades. Those making a trip to Hellsrun wore a red serpent armband they had received from the priests of the temples in their provinces to show their intentions were religious. Traveling merchants had to pay taxes as they entered each new province to buy protection and the opportunity to trade their goods.

As they rode along, Baqash thought how foolish it was for him to be making this trip. His heart was not in it. He did not accept Lucifer's authority over his life. He felt his father needed him to guard the province boundaries, and he could not stand the thought of being away from Landua for so long a time. Then he began to wonder what it would be like in Hellsrun. Would all the stories he had heard about the city be true—the vastness of her boundaries, the majesty of her great temple and the palaces of the almighty overlord Zuegan, the ruler of the largest province in the world? He had ruled longer than any other known warlord, some 300 revolutions around the sun. There was talk that Zuegan was making plans to bring all provinces of the world under his rule, creating a so-called one-world order. The thought caused Baqash to grit his teeth in anger.

One evening after traveling many miles, the two young travelers had stopped to take a night's rest. The stars shone brightly as they prepared to take turns sleeping and watching during the night. Megado walked back to the camp space, saying, "It's a good thing we stopped when we did. That laceration on my megalosaur's foot was getting worse. He should have enough time to heal by tomorrow sometime, but we may need to wait a few extra hours before we leave."

"That animal has always had soft feet," said Baqash angrily. "Some of these provinces do a bad job of keeping the rocks out of the roads as well. I guess we are just doomed to have these setbacks. It seems mighty Lucifer is going to fight me all the way to Hellsrun and back!"

Megado looked fearful and asked, his voice trembling, "Why do you have no fear of Lord Lucifer, Baqash, sir?"

"Ha!" laughed Baqash, his voice thick with cynicism. "You cannot fear one you hate so much. As a young boy, I had a sister who was the most beautiful woman I had seen. She took care of me as a child, and I loved her dearly. One day a Son of God appeared at the temple in our city and demanded her for a wife. My father tried to convince him that there were other women far fairer than she, but he would have no other. She was taken away and bore a daughter. They both were sacrificed at Hellsrun many revolutions ago."

"But sir, that is a great honor for your family," said Megado, his voice questioning.

"Honor?" yelled Baqash. "How can there be honor when grief smothers it like water on a fire? It was a far greater honor to see my sister's beauty every day than to see her taken away to have her life snuffed out to appease the ego of a god."

Megado turned and walked away from his fellow traveler, mumbling to himself, "I fear I have been linked to a man who may bring me much adversity. I pray Lucifer will understand my plight."

Later that night, as Baqash slept restlessly and Megado kept a bleary-eyed watch, a rustling sound came from the direction of where the megalosaurs were tied. Megado leapt to his feet and gave a cry of warning, but a hard blow to his head caused him to fall helplessly to the ground. Before Baqash could respond to Megado's yell, he felt a sharp, piercing pain just above his heart, and then a blow came to his head that left him unconscious and bleeding from his wounds.

Baqash finally began to come around in a dazed stupor as he heard a voice calling his name in a frantic fit of fear. When he slowly opened his eyes, he saw a serpent with its fangs still extended, staring him in the face. Megado had caught a viper in the forest and forced its venomous bite into the wound above Baqash's heart. The serpent venom had strong healing power; the bleeding stopped quickly, and the wound began to heal. Baqash was fortunate Megado had found a serpent so large and so quickly. The healing power in the bite of some of these creatures was one reason why they were held in such reverence. Some insects had similar powers as well.

"Oh, Master Baqash, I feared the knife had pierced your heart and that you were gone. Fortunately we are in a place where many serpents dwell. I have been a foolish servant who has allowed renegades to take our megalosaurs and leave us here for dead. Can you allow me to live, Master, for such a thing as this?"

Baqash did not respond as he lay there, still dazed from the blow to his head and the sharp pain in his chest. He gave himself a few moments to grasp his situation. As a prince and master of this slave, he had the right to put a sword into Megado for his negligence at watch, but then Baqash remembered that he had been vulnerable to Megado while he was unconscious, yet the slave had not taken his life. He also realized that Megado was still a young man who was not yet fully mature in the ways of war and survival. Baqash knew he had a long distance to travel, and Megado could still be of use to him if he learned from the great mistake.

Baqash rose to his knees and looked at the fear in the young man's eyes. With a growl of anger, he slapped the young man with his fist but then grimaced in pain and fell back to the ground, almost losing consciousness again. He knew he had to give the boy a jolt to let him know that he had made a mistake and that he was still under Baqash's authority and control.

When Baqash had regained some of his strength, he gritted his teeth in anger and said, "That is right, you foolish slave. You have made a terrible mistake, and I ought to put you to the sword right now. But instead I will let you live to remember your foolishness, and I will also make you work in the fields when we return to Madigan so that you can pay for the megalosaurs you have lost."

"Oh, Master!" cried Megado. "How will I ever overcome this mark on my life? I will always be known as the slave who let his master down!"

"Well," replied Baqash, still struggling to breathe, "that may be something you will have to answer for yourself. It may be that you will someday have the opportunity to redeem yourself, but as for now, find me some food to eat. Get me some water to drink to remove this thirst from my tongue, and then find some asper roots to take this pain from my head. And be quick about it."

The two men spent the rest of the day and night nursing their wounds. The deep wound in Baqash's chest would only take that long to heal fully in the dense atmospheric pressure. The serpent venom would hurry the process even more. They ate as many herbs, fruit, and berries as they could to build their strength for the long journey on foot to Hellsrun.

The next morning, as the sun's brilliant pink light reflected on the damp ground in the open spots of the forest floor, Baqash and Megado began their run to the north. They would pace themselves for runs of fifty miles every four hours of the day, taking short breaks between fifty-mile segments.

Baqash cursed his situation as he and Megado ran. He knew that unless they could find other megalosaurs or some other fast form of travel, his journey would take far longer than a single revolution around the sun. The thought of taking that long made him fearful for Landua and his father's province. He knew the Damogans would be ready to mount another attack before the end of another revolution. He also knew that Boax and some of Baqash's brothers might try a greedy overthrow of his father's authority in his province. If they were to succeed, it would mean certain death or banishment for Baqash and any others close to Cainogan, especially his close friend, Lemish, Landua's father.

As Baqash ran, his hatred for the serpent god grew stronger and stronger. He would not be making this trip it if weren't for this foolish requirement of all men. As he hurried along the roads of the beautiful fields and forests of the earth, he could not help but ponder ways to do away with the tyranny of this bloodthirsty god. Once in a while he ventured to think the impossible: that another God greater than Lucifer could possibly exist, a God that truly was as beautiful as the world that He had made.

The men ran for days, stopping to eat whatever the fields or forests around them yielded. They slept at the side of the roads they traveled, rising early and stopping late in the evening so as to make as much time as they could, for Baqash was a driven man. As they approached the center equatorial point of the earth, their fortunes were about to change.

One day as the two men ran, they were overtaken by a large battle wagon drawn by four magnificent triceratops. The two runners moved to the side of the road as the large wagon began to pass them by. But suddenly the driver did an unusual thing for road travel at that time: he called out and gave greetings as he pulled his team and the runners to a stop. Baqash and Megado gripped their weapons in preparation for a battle from whoever or whatever might be in the wagon.

"Fear not," laughed the huge man holding the reins that controlled the powerful beasts in their harnesses. "My name is Dago, and we mean you no harm."

"Who do you mean as we?" asked Baqash with firm suspicion. Strangers in those days were better left strangers. The motives of men were most often not based on a desire for the good of others.

"I assure you, you will not need your weapons this day although you are a little overmatched," smiled Dago as his huge arms glistened in the sunlight.

At that moment the door of the battle wagon swung open, and a man about the same size and age as Baqash stepped onto the road and faced the two runners. He was unusually dressed for a man riding in a battle wagon. He was wearing a robe like shepherds wear rather than the leather leggings, vest, and boots of a warrior. The thinly bearded stranger stood quietly for a moment, a slight smile on his face and strength and confidence in his bearing.

"I see you have met my friend and fellow traveler, Dago," he said casually. "My name is Adoniel. I can see by the bands on your arms that you are making your rite of passage journey to Hellsrun. We travel to Hellsrun as well. I thought by the way you have been running that your journey is urgent and that you and your slave could benefit by our faster mode of transportation."

"Yes, and how do you hope to benefit from us?" asked Baqash, still sternly gripping his sword. "We have already had our share of those who would help themselves to what belongs to others."

"Traveling the roads of the earth can be a dangerous endeavor. We only wish to give you aid. It is your choice to travel on alone if that be your desire," said Adoniel, turning to climb back into the wagon.

Baqash felt his suspicions lessen as this unassuming stranger prepared to leave. Baqash quickly remembered his desperate need to finish this journey and return home. He felt confident that he could handle himself against these men if they proved to be enemies. He had to take the chance. "I can tell you are a man for whom others have some level of respect, and as you say, I do have need to quicken my journey. My slave will ride with Dago," said Baqash defiantly, not wanting to show any sign of weakness to this man of strong but benevolent character.

Adoniel climbed into the battle wagon and left the door open behind him, as if to give welcome without a show of condescension. Baqash put away his sword as he climbed into the spacious traveling machine. Megado climbed up and sat next to Dago as the driver gave the triceratops the command to move on. With a huge lunge and the ease of a lion as it springs into a full run, the wagon jumped forward behind the awesome power of the large but swift beasts. Like the bear, the triceratops was as swift as a horse and could sustain a faster speed than man for a much longer time. Baqash would reach Hellsrun far more quickly if these strangers proved to have positive motives.

Three

Adoniel the Sethite

The battle wagon proved to be a fairly comfortable way to travel. It was spacious and covered with animal fur on the floor and walls. There were chairs and tables, and there were beds to lie on as the wagon rocked slightly on the smooth tile road. They were traveling in a province ruled by a very strong overload who kept his roads in good repair for defense purposes, for armies move more rapidly on well-kept roads.

Baqash did not speak for several miles. It seemed that Adoniel understood that his passenger would need some time to adjust to this new situation, so he left Baqash to himself and his thoughts. They had moved beyond the equatorial line and were traveling through the vast northern plains, which would take five hundred miles to pass through.

The plains were filled with vast herds of nomadic animals who roamed across the deep, thick grasslands. As Baqash looked out the bar-covered windows of the battle wagon, he saw mammoths, rhinoceroses, horses, elephants, giraffes, and all types of deer, antelope, and bison. There were not any of the larger dinosaur-type beasts because they preferred to inhabit the dense forests and lakes where they could eat the leaves of trees and shrubs and the marshy plants around and in the water.

Baqash finally spoke. "I noticed that you referred to the Holy Rite of Passage only as 'the Rite of Passage.' You make me think you are one who is not a religious man. That can be a dangerous way of life in a world controlled by a god like Lucifer."

"On the contrary," replied Adoniel, "I may be the most truly religious man you will ever meet." Adoniel paused to read Baqash's response before giving any further information. When he saw Baqash's eyes betray a glimmer of interest, Adoniel continued. "True religion is determined by how truth serves your God. Truth will not contradict the true God."

"That is one of the most dangerous statements I have ever heard spoken," said Baqash cautiously. "What your words tell me is that you do not accept the serpent as the true God. That is indeed a dangerous point of view—one I would think better kept to oneself. Should you be expressing this to a total stranger?"

"Yes, but you are not a stranger to me. The God I serve told me I would see a runner today who is a hater of the serpent god."

Baqash jumped to his feet and reached for his sword. Surely someone had betrayed his words of hate for Lucifer, and now this Adoniel had been sent to destroy him.

Before Baqash could draw his sword, Adoniel grabbed the loose fur carpets under the warrior's feet and gave them a jerk. Baqash was lifted off his feet, and Adoniel was upon him before he hit the floor. With one knee in his chest and a forearm across his neck, Adoniel put his face in Baqash's face and said sternly, "I live to give men life, not to take their lives away."

The force of this man's sincerity caused Baqash to go completely limp. He had never met a man like this one. The intensity in his eyes was not rage but something he had only seen once before, in an instant, in the eyes of his father during that unexpected embrace. In that moment, all of Baqash's suspicions melted away.

Adoniel stood and helped Baqash to his feet. The two men sat down in soft-padded chairs facing each other. Baqash waited to hear what Adoniel would say next.

"I am a Sethite, a son of Methuselah from the region of the Pishon, Gihon, Tigris, and Euphrates, often referred to as the Four Forks in the River. My grandfather is Enoch of the lineage of Seth. We are called the 'Line of Light,' for we are the protectors of the testimony of the one true Creator God, Elohim."

Baqash was without words. He had never before heard of this Line of Light. He had wished that another God could exist, a God who was greater than Lucifer, but until this moment he had never believed such a thing to be more than wishful thinking. He sat, staring in astonishment as he waited for this man to tell him more.

"I can tell these are new thoughts for you to consider, and so it is for most. Lucifer has worked hard to silence our message around the earth. For years we Sethites have had to live nomadic lives, always avoiding the searching eyes of Lucifer and his priests. But our God has kept us in His continual care. He is the One who told me of the hate in your heart."

"If you are such an enemy of Lucifer, then why to do you travel to Hellsrun, the very seat of his power?" asked Baqash with guarded interest. "Do you plan to satisfy the Holy Rite of Passage?"

"I would die before I made an oath to worship any god other than the one and true Elohim. I travel to Hellsrun to carry the message of the Line of Light to those who live in the deepest darkness. I will tell the true creation story to all who will listen," replied Adoniel with confident conviction.

"I am disappointed," said Baqash, a hint of sarcastic laughter in his voice. "Until now I thought you to be a man of much wisdom, but now you talk like a fool. To do what you say is to knowingly walk into a death trap."

"Who is the fool," asked Adoniel, not intimidated by Baqash's sarcasm, "the man who dies for living in the truth or the man who lives for accepting a lie?"

Baqash could feel anger and frustration swell in his chest. With gritted teeth he spoke, "How can a man know what the truth is in a world full of so many contradictions? The truth is that there is no truth except that I am alive and have learned to survive in a violent world. The truth is to survive."

"You can know the truth by what you see," replied Adoniel without hesitation. "Look around you. Could a god like Lucifer, who causes so much pain and suffering, even conceive of the beauty of this world, let alone create it? Could a god like Lucifer put emotions in the hearts of men who feel attraction to the beauty of a woman and the joy of viewing the acts of a child in its innocence before it learns to hate? But let me answer you something further. Could you deny the truth if you spoke to a man who had walked and talked with the true God and lived in a place of special creation that is now guarded by the fiery sword of God, a place that is guarded because of the existence of a special tree called the Tree of Life? These things and more are all there to be seen by those who want to live in the truth."

Adoniel had struck a chord in Baqash as he remembered his own battles with these very contradictions of beauty and love in a violent world. But these statements about a man and a garden and a special tree seemed far-fetched. "You speak like a man who has lost control of his great imagination. I would certainly have to see those things before I could accept them as true," said Baqash defensively.

"I will take you there myself after our work is done in Hellsrun," answered Adoniel, seeking agreement from Baqash.

"I do not have time to search for long-lost gardens and trees. As soon as possible I will return to my home, where I am needed even now. Maybe you will find those in Hellsrun who have time to waste on foolish adventures, but as for me, I have no interest in your offer and do not wish to speak more about it," replied Baqash, hoping to end this intimidating line of conversation.

"That is your choice, and it will be as you wish, but remember this one thing: the truth does not fear investigation." Adoniel abruptly ended the conversation.

As Adoniel and Baqash were discussing their very serious topics, Dago and Megado had already become good friends. Dago told Megado his life story—how he had been banished from his province because he had questioned the temple priests who had tried to take his land for themselves. They had tried to murder Dago as he and his family were fleeing to another city to gain help from family members. His own wife and children had been killed in the ambush, and he had been left for dead. Adoniel had come along and saved his life and taken him to his brother's city, but Dago found his family would have nothing to do with him because he had been falsely reported as an enemy of the temple. Adoniel had then invited Dago to join him, and since that time, Dago had become a follower of Elohim and a protector of the Line of Light.

Megado had told his new friend his story of growing up as a slave in the family of Cainogan and of his failure that had allowed his master's megalosaurs to be stolen. But Megado listened with great interest as Dago told him about the Line of Light and the Sethites who believed in the one true God, Elohim. "I would like to meet this man Adam and see this garden called Eden," he said in reply to Dago's testimony to the truth of Elohim.

The triceratops team had not slowed a step as the battle wagon moved swiftly down the tiled highway. The pavement began to turn to a clay-covered road as the travelers moved into another province. "I understand there is war in this province," said Dago as he looked around the landscape with concern in his eyes. "There is nothing worse than being caught in the middle of other men's wars."

Dago slowed the wagon when, in the distance, he saw smoke rising from what appeared to be a recent battleground. Adoniel opened the window under the driver's compartment and called out to Dago, "What do you see ahead?"

"This province is at war, and it looks as if a battle has taken place just ahead," Dago called back in a loud whisper. The last thing they needed was to be seen as the enemy by both sides.

Baqash had a thought. *This may be my chance to confiscate some megalosaurs and travel on to Hellsrun and rid myself of this madman.* He made a suggestion to Adoniel, "If you stop the wagon here, Megado and I will go on foot to scout out the battleground to see when it will be safe to move forward. We will then return to let you know it is safe to pass."

Adoniel was not surprised by Baqash's scheme, for he knew well the hearts of men. He would agree to let the men go, for they were not his captives, and he realized Baqash was not ready to accept his message of truth. His work had been accomplished and the seed had been planted, so he surrendered Baqash to a greater power as he replied, "Dago and I will wait for you here,"

Baqash moved out of the wagon and softly called, "Megado, come and go with me."

The two men slipped away on foot, moving quickly toward the battlefield. Megado whispered to his master, "What is your plan?" as he moved to Baqash's side.

"In battle there are often animals running free from the fallen masters. We may have a chance to mount two and run before we are detected," Baqash said excitedly.

"But what about our friends?" asked Megado.

"They are men of war like us; they will take care of themselves. They are on a dangerous journey, and we are wise to separate ourselves from them before we are identified with them."

Megado knew better than to question his master further, so he kept to himself his feeling of sadness at losing his new friend as they approached the battlefield, staying low in the grass a few yards from the road.

The time was approaching evening, and there were many cries of pain and deep groans of despair. The victors were still in pursuit of those who had fled the battle scene, though a few of the less wounded who remained behind on the battlefield mingled to finish off any of the enemy. These were not days of mercy. The more severely wounded victors were being taken to medicine wagons where the healing venoms of serpents and insects were being applied to the wounds. This was a perfect time for the two men to make their move: ahead lay a group of saddled megalosaurs that had been collected on the other side of the field.

"There they are," said Baqash as he pointed toward the megalosaurs. "We will sneak around and grab the two on the outside of the pack and flee on them across the field. Hopefully we will make it to the forest covering before any pursuers can overtake us. In the forest covering we will have a chance of escape."

They moved silently into position. The megalosaurs were loosely guarded. Baqash gave a nod, and both men jumped from the grass into the battle clearing. They then ran up to two of the megalosaurs and quickly mounted. They had bolted from the battlefield and were in full run before they were noticed by a group of guards, but out of the corners of their eyes they saw something they did not expect: a huge battle wagon was running among the guards, increasing their confusion and keeping them from acting. Baqash and Megado used this opportunity to ride quickly over a grassy hill and out of sight.

The two men rode across the plains long into the night. They passed through herds of animals, causing some to stampede in fear of the relentless riders. They planned to stay off the main road until they had distanced themselves from the warring province. They could follow the stars by night and the sun by day until they found their way back to another northbound highway.

They made it to the edge of the forest about an hour before dawn and decided to rest in the cover of the brush and towering trees. As they lay down, totally exhausted, they could not help but remember that they were free of any pursuers because of the intervention of the battle wagon. They now knew Adoniel and Dago were true friends. Baqash understood within his heart that Adoniel was not fooled by his scheme. *If I ever see that man again, he thought, I will hear more of what he has to say about this God, Elohim.* Baqash fell asleep with these thoughts running through his mind.

Four

The Damogan at Hellsrun

It took the travelers several more rotations from sun to moon, but they made their way back to a main northbound highway. They finally reached the border of the northernmost province—Zuegan, the largest and richest province in all the earth. Zuegan's highways were the best, and most who traveled for war had no place there. No other warlord would dare to test the strength of the greatest warlord, Zuegan, for whom the province was named. This warlord controlled the temple of Hellsrun and had the wealth to attract the most powerful Violent Ones. Zuegan knew the heads of all the monasteries that trained the Violent Ones, and he had the power and wealth to bring the strongest giants to his province.

It took Baqash and Megado another seven rotations to reach Hellsrun once they had crossed the border into Zuegan province. As the two men cleared the top of a high hill, they pulled their megalosaurs to a sudden stop. The sight before them was far more than they ever could have envisioned. There, sprawled before them for miles and miles, was the mighty city of Hellsrun. As they sat speechless on their mounts, they could see the towering Temple of the Serpent, which covered a square mile in the very middle of the vast metropolis.

"Well, Megado, there it is. We have finally achieved our goal," said Baqash as Megado continued to take in the awesome sight.

"Yes, and the sooner we can do our business and return to Madigan, the better I will feel. I do not feel good about being in this place," Megado answered, a note of fear in his voice. The things that Dago had told Megado had begun to take root in his heart.

The two travelers rode into the city cautiously, not knowing what to expect. They had heard that the temple provided rooms for the men who came for the Holy Rite of Passage, so they rode straight to the temple. It was not hard to find, for it towered above all other buildings in the city.

The streets were full of people. There were many meeting places where men could go to embrace every pleasure, and music and laughter spilled from every building. Crowds of people surrounded open-air arenas in which either men or women fought in blood-ridden contests. The roar of a huge crowd came from a 100,000-seat arena that was close to the temple area. The crowd roared for those prisoners who battled for their lives against a Violent One or a behemoth that had been trained to be a vicious, bloodthirsty killer. The tyrannosaurus behemoth was normally a docile, giant plant eater, not a hunting killer. Only man could make a behemoth a killer.

It is no wonder that many men who come here never return home, Baqash thought. *They come here and want to stay rather than return to responsible lives back home.* It was sad to think that many who stayed were forced into slavery or the army or murdered by those whom they thought were friends. Only a few ever made their way as productive members of the community.

The two young men stopped in front of a building connected to the temple that looked like a place where men might stay. Megado remained with the megalosaurs as Baqash went inside. Several men wearing red serpent armbands sat in a large room, talking and cursing in loud voices. These were men from all over the earth who had made the journey to fulfill their Holy Rite of Passage. Baqash noticed a man who wore the markings of the Damogans. He knew he must keep his eye on this man.

Baqash looked around the room for a temple priest who might tell him how to make arrangements for a room. He spied one standing by a group of men, so he walked over to introduce himself to the priest. The priest turned to look Baqash in the eye. He was a large, stoutly built man with hair pulled atop his head like a horse's tail. His eyes were red as they glared from a face painted in white and black stripes. He looked at Baqash and sized him up as a man would lust for a woman. Baqash had expected that kind of response from the priest, for most were lovers of men rather than women.

"Who are you?" asked the priest, his voice deep and full.

"I am Baqash of the province of Cainogan. My slave and I are in need of lodging while we fulfill the Holy Rite of Passage."

"You will need to follow me. I will show you to your barracks. This is not a place of leisure; you may find that in the city. Men sleep on the floor in bedrolls they must provide for themselves. There is a place to bathe and clean your clothes at the end of the barracks. Men are required to do their own cleaning and to provide their own food. There is to be no fighting in the temple area, and any thief will be put to death immediately. We don't fool with those who cause trouble when they come here. Remember, you are on holy ground." The priest showed Baqash to a long, narrow room that already had several bedrolls laid out along each side of the room.

Baqash left the priest and went outside to where Megado stood with the megalosaurs. "We will find an animal caretaker and leave the animals there until we are ready to leave this place," he said as he and Megado mounted. Baqash did not want to keep the animals on the street any longer than necessary for fear that someone might recognize the battle trappings from their province and accuse them of thievery.

Later that evening, the two men found a place of pleasure for food and drink. There were women and men for the entertainment of those who would barter for it, but Baqash had decided it best to stay away from possible entanglements. He was there only to finish that for which he had come. And since his encounter with Adoniel, there was also something that had lessened his desire to pursue such things. For some reason things were no longer the same. Baqash was not the same.

As they ate their food and sipped the strong wine, Baqash noticed the Damogan warrior leaving the place of pleasure. He had two men with him, and it was obvious they were under the influence of the strong wine. As Baqash watched them leave, he saw the warrior look at him in a way that made Baqash sense that he had not seen the last of the man. At that moment Baqash realized that the Damogan knew who he was.

Quickly Baqash reached over and took from Megado his wine.

When the slave looked with questioning eyes, Baqash said, "I have a feeling we will need to keep our heads clear of wine this night." Megado turned his head and watched with his master as the three men walked out into the night.

The sky was filled with the brilliant light of the stars, and the full moon loomed like a giant glimmering pearl. Baqash and Megado were careful to keep watch as they walked along the street that led back to the temple barracks. Not being familiar with the layout of the city, it was hard for them to know where their enemies might try to make their move.

Even though the hour was late, the streets remained full of people and would do so until the last person succumbed to the sleep of too much wine. Many still mingled outside the places of pleasure that lined the street, and it was from the midst of a group of these loiterers that three men stepped into the street to stand face to face with Baqash and Megado. The Damogan was the largest of the three, and he stood in the middle. The men were somewhat larger than the Cainogans, but Baqash and Megado's clear heads made them more than a match for these brutes. As they faced their enemy, Baqash knew he had to kill the Damogan. He could not allow the man to take word back to his leaders that Baqash was not in the Cainogan province.

The Damogan spoke first. "I know you, you worthless excuse for a piece of flesh. You are Baqash, the son of the warlord Cainogan. Tonight I will split your skull, and tomorrow I will leave for Damogan to receive my reward for your filthy scalp. I will tell them the mighty right arm of Cainogan has fallen, and the province is ours for the taking!"

Baqash grinned, for he knew this drunken fool had fallen into his hands. *No one will miss him at the temple,* he thought. *They will all think he is returning to Damogan.* As for his two friends, when they wake up in the morning, this night will be only a blur. They will merely feel the knots on their skulls and the throbbing in their heads from too much wine. He looked to his side and saw a dark passage between two buildings. He knew when he yelled "right flank," Megado would know what to do.

Baqash made his move. "Right flank!" he yelled, leaping for the cover of darkness. Megado sprang like a cheetah on the heels of Baqash, as though he had been reading his mind. All the years of battle training Baqash had given him kicked in like a natural instinct. The two Cainogans were in the passage almost before the thugs could react. With clear heads they would have known better than to fall into this trap, but wine has a way of making men do foolish things.

The drunken Damogan hit the dark passage first, clumsily pulling on his sword to get it out of its sheath. Baqash finished him with one well-placed blow of his own sword across the warrior's chest. The other two brutes came into reach close behind. Megado dealt a crushing blow to the head of the one closer to him, and Baqash freed his sword and spun just in time to bring the butt of his sword handle across the third man's face. The enemy men fell limp to the ground and lay moaning, not knowing what had hit them.

Megado looked out into the street to see if anyone was aware or even cared about what had just happened. They had not been detected. They left the two men lying in a heap as they carried the Damogan warrior's body down the dark passage to find a place to dispose of him. They came to the river that ran behind the temple, the river into which the blood of the sacrifices was washed. It was accustomed to washing away the evidence of man's bloody hands.

Baqash and his slave tied weights to the body and pushed it into the river. In time, the undercurrent would carry it to the sea. As Baqash hurriedly moved away from the river with Megado close behind, somehow he did not feel the swell of victorious pride he would have felt not long ago. The humiliation he had just inflicted on his enemy had not brought exhilaration as it had before. *What has happened to me?* he thought as they moved quickly in the dark. *This man, Adoniel, has put a secret spell on me!*

Five

A Life-Changing Experience

It would be several rotations before Baqash and Megado were ready to take their final vows of submission to Lucifer, kiss the head of the serpent, and receive their mark. They would be taught the many secrets of the serpent and learn the dark ceremonies of the temple. During their training sessions Baqash often daydreamed about Landua and her beauty. He recalled their times together in her father's garden when they had hidden from Falenish and stolen a kiss or two. He often remembered his father and the possible attack of the Damogans or an overthrow by his ambitious older brothers. Baqash also kept hoping his father would rid himself of the Violent One, Boax. He had heard the Damogans were not successful in wooing a Violent One from Hellsrun. They could not offer enough wealth to make it worth a move from the greatest city in the world.

Soon it was the day before Baqash and Megado were to finally say their vows of submission and finish their Holy Rite of Passage. They had heard there was going to be a special event at the sports arena: a great enemy of Lucifer was to be executed by facing a killer behemoth. The two men decided to attend this spectacle before returning to Madigan, for the arena in Hellsrun was as famous worldwide as the temple. They had to experience it at least one time before they left Hellsrun for good.

It was afternoon. Several prisoners had already battled to the death. The victors had to win three matches in an annual revolution and then defeat a Violent One or a killer behemoth in order to earn their freedom. Very few ever did, and none had on this day. Several prisoners opted to work as slaves the rest of their lives rather than face the arena, but those who were judged as enemies of Lucifer in the temple had no choice. They had to fight in the arena. If they won their freedom, then it was understood that Lucifer had allowed them a reprieve.

The final event of the day was a judgment against an enemy of the highest kind. This man would face the killer behemoth without a revolution of battles, and if by some amazing turn of events he defeated the giant beast, then he would immediately face the most powerful Violent One in Hellsrun, Hercineolas. The man would be allowed one weapon of his choice against either opponent. The Violent One could use all the weapons he desired to use.

Instead of the regular priest of the arena, the high priest was to introduce this prisoner. He would declare the man's offenses and then announce his name. This man was gaining a strong following, so the high priest desired to make him an example and disperse any possible movement that might develop among those he had corrupted.

The gigantic doors at the end of the arena opened. A man, escorted by two powerful warriors on each side, began a slow but deliberate walk into the center of the high-walled court, which was surrounded by seating rising steeply into the air in such a way that every spectator could see by looking almost straight down. The stands were packed with yelling, jeering, bloodthirsty men and women. They cursed, threatened, and yelled obscenities at this man, though few had any idea who he was. The man was undaunted by the crowd and showed no signs of fear. Baqash and Megado sat at the opposite side of the arena as they watched the man and his escort move toward the center. When he reached the center point, he stopped and faced the crowd, looking straight into the stands. In stunned unison Baqash and Megado whispered, "Adoniel!"

Adoniel turned and faced the high priest and waited for his accusations to be declared. The priest stood and walked to the edge of the high-walled court, which stood as tall as the head of a killer behemoth. A protective iron fence kept the combatants away from the wall of the court so that all spectators could watch the excitement. The high priest stood for several minutes and with a great deal of satisfaction glared down at his prized prisoner. He waited in his lush, jewel-laden robes as the crowd became silent.

One hundred thousand humans became completely quiet as the high priest began to speak. "Worshipers of the one and only true god, the mighty giver of all life, most holy and just, our great serpent god, Lucifer, hear me. This man is a blasphemer who would turn the hearts of worshipers unto himself. He is a deceiver telling stories to defile the truth. This man has made his way into the homes of the unwary to deceive them with his lies. All who have heard him have turned from him, and now he stands alone. Today you will see how men who stand against our great and mighty god die in their guilt. Today the name of this man will become a byword around the whole world, for men will say from this day forward, 'May you be cursed of Lucifer just as the fool called Adoniel.'"

As those words echoed around the arena, the crowd rose and erupted in a mighty roar of exaltation to the serpent. Adoniel's guard reached over and released his arms from behind his back. His chosen weapon was wrapped around his waist. It was a long cord of interlaced goat leather. Two large, round, smooth rocks encased in a web of leather were bound to each end of the cord. It was a very strange weapon that, heretofore, no one at the arena had ever seen.

The guards ran to the gate of escape in the iron fence and locked it behind them. Adoniel knelt slowly in the dust and bowed his head in a position of submission. As he knelt, the gigantic doors began to open again, and a huge beast butted his head against them impatiently so as to thrust them apart more quickly. The doors finally parted wide enough to let the giant killer behemoth into the arena court. The beast roared as it burst into the court, running nervously around the iron fence as it prepared to attack its prey. The animal stood twenty feet tall on two powerful lower legs, while its upper legs were like tiny arms, almost useless. It was forty-five feet long from the top of its head to the end of its long tail. Its head was four feet long, and its large mouth was lined with eight-inch dagger-like teeth that could cut a man in half with one ferocious bite. This was the killer behemoth.

The animal was not tentative before it prepared to attack

because it was not by nature a vicious animal. Its kind normally roamed the forests, using their teeth to strip leaves and bark from branches high in trees. The behemoth, like all other animals, would attack a man or another beast only if it felt threatened by their presence. Men had learned that they could train the behemoths to be killers by harsh treatment and food deprivation. When the animal became hungry enough, it could be taught to eat meat and be attracted to the smell of blood. The behemoth became a killer only after it learned to prefer a blood and meat diet, and in captivity that was all the animal was given to eat. It was a killer because it was no longer normal. Instead it was, by man's design, a freak of nature.

The killer behemoth slowed to a walk after a few circles around the arena court. The ground shook from the jarring of its tremendous, talon-laden, three-toed feet. Its eyes finally fell on the man kneeling in the center of the ring. The beast gave a thunderous roar and began to stalk its prey while the crowd yelled ever more loudly in gleeful, expectant bloodlust. It was obvious the killer behemoth had not been fed for quite some time.

As the huge animal walked closer to the man on his knees, it could hear Adoniel calmly singing a song. The crowd quieted in amazement as the beast hesitated, looking down at Adoniel. Slowly the man stood before the behemoth and faced it, still softly singing. The godly man had been taught from childhood that in the creation record, Elohim had given man dominion over all the earth, including all its creatures. Adoniel had been asking God to allow him to reclaim that lost dominion for this time of testimony.

He slowly reached in his coat and pulled out some leaves he had collected before being taken into custody. Adoniel knew the animal had a natural attraction to their smell; this would confuse its lust for blood and cause the behemoth to become docile. As Adoniel continued to sing, he continually looked the animal in the eye until it fell into a hypnotic trance. In several minutes, the killer behemoth slowly lay down and went to sleep.

Stunned in total amazement, the crowd had never witnessed this kind of power before. As Adoniel stood before the sleeping giant, he bowed his head in thanksgiving to his God. The crowd stood and cheered approvingly. The high priest quickly jumped to his feet and gave the signal to call in Hercineolas, the most renowned Violent One in all of Hellsrun. There may have been others greater on the earth, but none had yet gained the fame of the strength and power of Hercineolas.

The crowd remained on its feet to see how this amazing warrior would stand against the great Violent One. Hercineolas ran into the arena in full battle dress, wielding sword, spear, and shield. He had been told he would receive many great rewards if he did away with the blasphemer. The giant stood fifteen and a half feet tall and dwarfed Adoniel, who was only eight feet tall. He looked like a small boy gazing up at a very large man. As the giant ran into the court for battle, Adoniel unwrapped his weapon of choice from around his waist.

Hercineolas stopped in his tracks when he saw the strange sight before him: a killer behemoth lying asleep on the ground and an average-sized man standing near it, getting ready to swing around his head a cord with rocks tied at each end. The sight struck him as humorous, and he stood for a moment, lowered his weapons, and began to laugh. Adoniel seized the moment, and with a loud cry he yelled, "In the name of Elohim!" He released the goat leather weapon that was in full swing above his head.

The center of the thick cord hit the giant directly in the throat before he could react. Adoniel had thrown the weapon with such force that the stones at the end of the cord tightly wrapped the leather strap about the neck of the Violent One. The cord was so tight that it completely cut off his breathing.

Hercineolas fell to the ground, frantically thrashing. He was unaware that Adoniel had quickly seized his sword, and he rolled over on his back, pulling desperately on the goat leather cord. Hercineolas looked up just in time to see Adoniel bring the sword down across his neck with all the force in his body. The mighty warrior giant was dead.

The high priest fell back into his chair in shock as the crowd went wild in a fit of delirious excitement. Adoniel fell to his knees once again to give thanks to his God, Elohim. He then stood before the massive crowd and signaled for silence. Slowly the crowd ceased its cheering for this great hero, who was standing between a sleeping killer behemoth and a dead Violent One.

When the crowd was quiet, Adoniel took his stand for his God, speaking out so the crowd could hear. "I am Adoniel, the son of Methuselah, of the lineage of Seth, the son of Adam, the father of us all who was made in the image of the one true God, Elohim. I want you to know that it is my God, Elohim, Creator of us all, who has delivered me this day from the hand of the fallen angel, Lucifer. I have been sent by my God to give witness this day so that all who have seen and heard will know that there is no other God that we must serve but Elohim. He is the God who is the Creator and Sustainer of all things…"

Adoniel stopped short and stiffened as five arrows struck him in the back. He stood for a moment, pointed his finger to the heavens, and made a final cry of victory: "Elohim!" Then he fell to his knees and toppled face down in the dirt as blood ran from his wounds and trickled to the ground. The high priest had gathered himself together and signaled for his archers stationed behind Adoniel to silence the truth.

The high priest then yelled in self-justifying anger, "The blasphemer is dead!" A hush fell over the arena, and the people stood confused and bewildered, looking at the scene in the middle of the arena court. Was this man a blasphemer or was he a hero? The behemoth awakened and stood. It walked over to where Adoniel lay and leaned over the body as if to mourn a fallen master.

Baqash and Megado had no questions in their minds as they stood stunned and outraged. They knew in their hearts that they had just witnessed a true expression of real power. They realized they had never seen such courage before, born by a faith they had never known. They would never be the same men again. They also knew that they could not take the vows of submission to the serpent or receive the mark of Lucifer. Instead they would flee from Hellsrun that night and become enemies of Lucifer.

As they left the arena to make preparations for their escape, Baqash and Megado overheard a group of people talking. Apparently they had been a part of some of Adoniel's secret sessions that had led to his arrest. In the conversation it was stated that Adoniel had a servant named Dago who would face a killer behemoth the next day, just as Adoniel had done today. With this information in mind, the two men went and packed their belongings as though to make preparation to leave the day after the ceremonies. They brought the megalosaurs to the barracks and loaded them with their possessions. Then they went back to the arena to find a way to free Dago.

The prison lay under the huge arena, and they had no idea where Dago might be. He was probably isolated in a cell, separated from all prisoners, and had little contact with any guards. It was possible that the high priest would have Dago killed secretly rather than risk the possibility of another exhibition like the one Adoniel had given earlier that day. He did not need anything to happen that might incite the people to revolt.

With all these considerations in mind, the two Cainogan liberators made their way to the deepest and darkest part of the prison. Lining the walls there were wine electrolysis lamps, several feet apart. It was very damp that far underground, and there were sounds of dripping water like those heard in caves. Baqash and Megado hid in nooks and crannies to avoid passing guards, but they finally decided to take on two passing guards and borrow their uniforms. It was the only way to find Dago. They waited for the next two guards to pass their hiding place. They were able to club the two men into unconsciousness and drag them out of sight. Baqash and Megado then tied them with their boot laces and stuffed cloth in their mouths. The guards never knew what hit them. They would be put in prison themselves the next day for being negligent.

Baqash and Megado made their way quickly to the end of the prison in the very bottom level. They found a guard post there and asked for the prisoner, Dago. To their relief, the guard replied, "He is here, but what would you want of him?"

"We have been sent by the high priest. He has plans for him," replied Baqash.

"What is the secret password?" asked the guard suspiciously. He looked Baqash straight in the eye and did not notice as Megado hit him with his fist across his jaw. The guard was unconscious before he hit the floor. The two men grabbed the key and went immediately to the isolation cell in the circle of cells surrounding them.

As they opened the door, Dago jumped to his feet in surprise. Megado spoke in a low whisper, "Do not fear, Dago. It is your friend, Megado."

Dago could not believe his eyes when he recognized the young slave and his master. "What are you doing here?" he said with restrained joy, knowing guards would soon be coming.

"We will explain later. Come with us while there is still time," demanded Baqash, feeling the pressure of the moment. They dragged the guard into the cell and locked the door. Dago put his arms behind his back, and the two disguised warriors escorted him out of the prison, walking quickly and talking roughly so as not to be hindered by passing guards.

When the three men came out of the prison, they ran to where the megalosaurs were waiting and mounted quickly, Dago climbing behind Megado. They rode away to a safer place where they could stop and explain the situation.

In a clump of trees while the night lights shone at the outer edge of Hellsrun, Baqash told Dago their story. They told of their decision to not take the oath of submission and their plans to make their way back to Madigan. They invited Dago to join them in their journey.

Dago was overcome with grief as he heard his friends tell of Adoniel's valiant death. His body shook as the very large man wept over the loss of his dear friend. After several minutes he regained composure and lifted his head to speak. "Now I know what he meant when he said he must give his witness in Hellsrun. I thought he meant he would work in secret, but now I see that he knew this would be his end from the time he committed to come." He paused for a moment and then spoke again. "No, I cannot go with you to your people. I must return to the people of Adoniel and tell his father of his son's great sacrifice for the truth of his God, Elohim. There are people here in Hellsrun who can help me make my way back to the land of the Four Forks in the River. You go your way, and I will go mine. And may Elohim give you His covering."

Baqash and Megado did not try to change their friend's mind. They knew what he said was right. They gave him a strong-armed embrace, which he returned as they all realized the common bond they had found through their friend, Adoniel.

The two changed men mounted their beasts and rode away

into the night, not knowing what lay ahead but knowing they must one day find the garden and read the words of the creation record protected by the Line of Light.

Six

The Long Ride Home

There was no time to waste as Baqash and Megado ran their megalosaurs relentlessly along the highways and back roads. They knew that the temple in Hellsrun would send word to the temple in Madigan—and all along the way back to the Cainogan province. They were already hunted men, so they did all they could to avoid any encounters with strangers of any kind. They kept to themselves by sleeping in wooded areas and eating wild fruit, berries, and vegetables; the megalosaurs grazed on plants and tree leaves. There were plenty of clear-flowing streams for them to find water whenever they needed refreshment.

Baqash fought the battle of second thoughts as he traveled the long stretches of road between their infrequent stops for food and sleep. He thought of facing his father and Lemish, as well as Landua, and then wondered if he had done the right thing. Maybe he should have taken the vows even if he did not mean them. It would have made his life so much easier. But then he saw pictures in his mind of Adoniel's mighty exhibition of power and remember his question: Who is the fool—one who lives a lie or one who dies for the truth?

Regardless of what the response would be back home, Baqash felt driven to get there as soon as possible. A revolution had almost passed, and he sensed within himself that something terrible was going to happen if he did not return home soon. There was the possibility of a family revolt or another attack by the Damogans. The Violent One, Boax, would also need to be dealt with if his father had not already done so. Baqash hoped that even though he would not be able to stay in Cainogan province because he was now an enemy of Lucifer, he could help his father strengthen his power once again before having to leave. He also hoped that by some twist of fate, he could still take Landua with him.

It was late in the evening when Baqash and Megado pulled their beasts to a stop. The bridle on the animal was wrapped around the megalosaur's mouth so that it would not try to stop and eat. Two hooks, extending from the mouth strap, were placed in the animal's nostrils to cause enough pressure to make it turn. Their short necks took too much leverage to turn their heads with a bit like those used for the less efficient horse and donkey. The remainder of the bridle was made up of the nostril straps, which extended through the mouth strap and over the head. The reins were attached to the nostril hooks to apply pressure for turning. The saddle had a high back for the rider to lean on while his mount was standing upright. When the rider spurred the animal in the ribs, the megalosaur leaned forward and straightened his tail while his powerful back legs ran like a precision machine. The rider leaned forward, pushing his feet toward the rear of the beast, almost lying on the reptile's neck. The saddle extended up the neck for the rider to have a place on which to lean forward.

When the beasts stopped, their riders swung out of their saddles and stepped to the ground, walking around a bit to allow the animals to adjust after their long run. They found a place in the trees off the road to allow the animals to eat; they could also drink from a nearby stream. The two men tied the animals to a large tree and walked around the forest, collecting nuts and berries and wild vegetables. They both looked forward to the time when they could eat prepared breads and cakes and again drink cold mammal milk. They rolled out their bedrolls on the ground, careful to place them so they would be out of reach of the wandering megalosaurs, each of whom had one leg tied by a long leather rope. The beasts would be free to eat and drink all night without wandering off.

After a time of conversation, the two weary travelers lay down to sleep. They were far enough away from any civilization to be free from worry about keeping guard in the night.

It was Baqash who woke first when he heard a terrible sound moving toward their camp. Trees were moving and shaking and falling down several yards away. The ground shook with continuing thuds that were becoming heavier and more frequent. As Baqash looked above the tree line in the starlit night, he realized what was coming their way. Megado had also heard the rumbling in the forest and jumped to his feet.

"Quick! Untie the animals!" yelled Baqash as he ran around, trying to gather up their gear.

"What is it?" Megado cried as he ran to untie the megalosaurs.

"Just cut them loose! Let them run, and then grab some gear!

There is not much time! We have to get out of here fast!" Baqash yelled as he frantically filled his arms with as much as he could carry.

By now Megado could see what was coming. In the tops of the trees he could see the heads of fifty or more brachiosaurs weaving and bobbing as they moved as fast as they could toward the camp. The fifty heads moving high in the shaking trees meant that at least another thirty newborns and yearlings that could not be seen were following. Anything in their path would be trampled into unidentifiable mush.

It was all the men could do to get out of the path of the herd as they migrated to another feeding ground several miles away. The noise was deafening as the magnificent four-legged giants moved past the fleeing men. Their calls, which emanated from the tops of their heads, sounded like horns and were effective in helping the animals stay together and prevent the young ones from straying from the adult circle of females that followed the lead bulls. They kept themselves in formation as they moved forward, unhindered by any obstacles.

Baqash and Megado barely escaped the thundering thuds of feet that were as big as the base of a tree. There was nothing they could do but sit and wait until the stampede of mountain-sized beasts moved by. They shuddered as it dawned on them how close they had come to being crushed under the massive weight of one of the gigantic beasts.

They walked back across the newly made clearing as they began their search for their two megalosaurs. The path the brachiosaurs had made was seventy yards wide. There were trees more than a hundred feet tall lying on the ground, completely uprooted, with branches torn off and trampled into the forest floor.

The megalosaurs would not be too far away since they had become highly dependent on their masters from having been in captivity for a long period of time. They would still have their leather ropes tied to a leg and would be limited in their movement. The men hoped the animals had not become tangled in the brush as they fled from the brachiosaur herd.

It took about two long sundial degrees of precious time before the animals could be located and settled down. They rested a few more degrees and then resaddled and started on their fast-paced journey home. They headed back to the main highway, deciding they would rather take a chance of being seen by temple priests than losing any more time traveling on back roads and across the herd-ridden plains.

Once they were back on the highway, the two men traveled for several hours until they saw a caravan moving toward them. It was one of the very large caravans that made their way north from the south and then back south again, carrying every kind of item imaginable. These caravans could be found traveling all over the world, going to any place of consequence unless hindered by province wars or marauding thieves. They were a tremendous source of information about the places they had already been because they stopped in all the major cities and towns to buy, trade, and pay road-use tolls.

With the caravan were a couple of miles of all kinds of pachyderms lined up one behind another. There were mammoths, elephants, triceratops, horses, donkeys, and camels of all kinds. Some carried large packs on their backs; others pulled heavily loaded wagons. Traders rode on the wagons or on their loaded beasts. While some walked alongside the caravan, others rode their own mounts. There were always a number of hired warriors to travel with the caravans for protection. Those who traveled in the caravans made it a total way of life. They lived and had families and died traveling around the world, usually on the same route going to and from where they had just been.

The two riders slowed their megalosaurs as they approached the leader of the caravan. "Long life to you," said Baqash to the caravan master.

"Long life indeed," said the master jovially, hoping he might have a buyer for something he had to sell. "Where do you men travel so hard that your beasts show signs of being sorely driven?"

"We travel to the Cainogan province city called Madigan," replied Baqash, a smile on his face so as not to cause the captain to be suspicious of them. They pulled their animals to a walk beside the mammoth on which the master was riding in an intricately carved wooden riding carriage, covered with soft leather and plush woolen rugs. The caravan master had become very rich traveling the earth. "Do you have any news of Madigan?" asked Baqash, squinting. He had to look up into the sun at mid-day to look the master in the eye.

"News always comes with a price," said the master with a sly grin. "What is the news worth to you?"

"I need gifts to take to my father and my betrothed," answered Baqash in playful hesitation, expecting that the master would try to sell him something. "What would you suggest?"

"I have a hand-woven gold necklace for the beautiful lady and a handsome ring that would bring respect to the finger of any great man." The master reached into a box he had in his carriage and brought out the merchandise for Baqash to see.

"They are very fine pieces of handiwork. I'll take them," said Baqash as he reached for the pouch inside his belt. He brought out a gold coin and a few silver coins and handed them to the master.

The master looked at Baqash with a grin and said, "One more silver dagon, and they are yours." The caravan master was taking advantage of Baqash, but then he was buying information that was well worth the difference in value.

The caravan master handed over the jewelry. Baqash took the stone and raised it to look at it in the pink hue of sunlight. The master grinned when he knew he had made a bargain and began to speak. "Madigan is a troubled placed. You do well to hurry there. Cainogan, the lord of the province, has overthrown two of his sons who tried to take over the province. In the process the Violent One who was in allegiance to Cainogan has defected to the Damogans, who apparently have offered him more rewards than Cainogan was willing to pay. We could not stay long in Madigan, but we heard rumors that the Damogans would soon be mounting an attack. As we traveled through part of Damogan, we saw signs that the rumors were true. There was an army collecting in Damogan, and it is probably already moving toward Madigan by now."

With those words still ringing in their ears, the two Cainogans spun their mounts around and headed south at a full run. Their greatest fears had been confirmed, and there was no need to continue their conversation any further. They had to reach Madigan as soon as possible, even though it meant they must take shorter rests and run in longer increments of time. They could make it home in another three rotations at that pace. They hoped it would not be too late.

Seven

The Pain of Broken Dreams

The Damogan army had already reached the hills that surrounded Madigan by the time the two warriors reached the outskirts of the city. Apparently the Damogan army had been able to resist frontal attacks by the Cainogans and had forced them to retreat to the walled city fortress. They waited until dark before they made a run for the city walls, for they would have to break through a part of the Damogan ranks to do so. Baqash knew the signal he could make to the guards on the wall so they would know to let him and Megado enter.

As the army was bedding down and changing the guard, Baqash and Megado rode through the camp at full speed. The Damogan warriors were caught by surprise, and the two men were halfway to the gates before the guards could mount their animals and enter the chase. If the pursuers came too close to the city, they would be picked off by archers on the wall, so they gave up before they even got started. Baqash gave the appropriate arm signals as they rode up to the city wall, and the gates opened as some of the guards recognized who was signaling them.

"It's Baqash!" several said in unison as the two riders entered the city and the gates closed behind them. They rode straight to Caino-gan's house, knowing that his father would be making plans with his leaders to try to withstand the Damogan attacks.

The two men jumped from their megalosaurs as they stopped in front of the sculptured mansion. "Wait here," Baqash commanded Megado, returning to his leadership role over his father's forces. He ran into the house and straight to his father's conference room. He could not wait to see his father's joy that his youngest son was back in time to help bring about another deliverance from this ever-present enemy. He did not hesitate as he opened the double doors to hurry in and get to business.

But Baqash was not ready for what he was to encounter next. As he barged into the room, his father looked up, as did the men around him. They merely stood and stared, their reaction telling Baqash that his father and the men around him were not happy to see him. "Father?" queried Baqash, a puzzled look on his face.

"Leave us," said Cainogan to the men standing around him. He continued to stare at his puzzled son. The men complied, walking past Baqash without giving him a glance. Baqash turned and closed the doors behind him and then faced his father, bracing himself for whatever was to come.

"Baqash, you promised me you would go through the Holy Rite of Passage. The temple priests have come several times looking for you and Megado. If I do not turn you in, they will excommunicate my whole family from the temple. The Damogans have taken heart against us, and Boax has defected to them because they feel the temple priest and the rest of the people will turn against me as a result of your foolish rebellion against Lucifer. You are a grave disappointment to me, and I can never forgive you for what you have done."

Baqash knew in his heart that he could not try to convince his father to hear his explanation. It was obvious that he had been unable to return to Madigan before the Hellsrun priests had sent word of his rebellion to the local priests. He had brought danger to his father's house by returning. He knew he would have to run, and he knew he would have to do it in a way that would make it look like his father had tried to abduct him. He quickly turned, threw open the doors, and ran out in the midst of the waiting men, yelling back at his father, "Do you think I'm going to stay here and let you turn me over to the temple priests?"

"Grab him!" cried Cainogan as his son turned to run.

Two men ran toward Baqash to take hold of him, but he was too quick as he dodged one, knocked the other down, and spun for the door. He jumped out into the night, leaping into his saddle as Megado followed suit. They took off down the paved street and then ducked behind some buildings as a group of warriors ran past.

Baqash had one more stop to make before he left Madigan. He had to see if Landua would leave with him. The two fugitives made their way down back streets until they came to Landua's house. Baqash knew well the window where Landua's room was. He had often seen her looking out the window over the years when he had come to visit her; her habit was to wait at her window to see him come to the house. He would never have tried to make his way to that room in times past because that would have ruined his opportunity to finally have Landua for his own. Now it seemed he had nothing to lose by at least trying to see Landua one more time before he left the province.

Baqash climbed up the large vines that grew on the wall under Landua's window. He looked in the open window to see his love sitting on a chair with her head in her hands, crying. He climbed into the room and whispered her name, trying not to startle her. She gasped in surprise and stood up to yell, thinking she was under attack. Then she recognized who was in her room.

"Baqash!" she cried with relief and a hint of joy as she resisted the urge to run into his arms and kiss him. The priests had made their visit here as well. Baqash moved to her, knowing she would not resist him. He took her in his arms and kissed her, but she did not receive the kiss. Instead she turned away and began to cry again.

Baqash spoke in desperation, "Landua, I don't have much time. I have to leave the city. Father wants to turn me in to the temple priests, and I can't let him do that. I have come to ask you to leave with me..."

"Before he could finish, Landua began to laugh hysterically. "You want me to go with you? Where are we going to go? Who will allow an enemy of Lucifer to live peacefully anywhere? What kind of life would we have, running not only from the priests of Lucifer but also from my father and his avenging anger? No, Baqash, I cannot, I will not go with you."

"Landua, listen to me," Baqash pleaded. "There is a place where we can go. There are people who will take us in and let us live in peace. I am going to a land where I can find the truth, and if you go with me, you can find the truth, too…"

"Truth!" Landau interrupted, almost screaming. "What do you know about the truth? The truth was that I loved you, and I trusted you, and I waited for you, and you did not keep your word. No, I will not go with you. There is no life left for us together. Get out before my father hears us and kills you for invading his house like a common thief!" She turned and ran to the door as though she were going to call for help. Baqash had no choice but to jump out the window and leave Landua behind. Tears were streaming from his eyes as he made his way back to Megado and the megalosaurs. The pain in his heart was almost unbearable as he tried to think through his next move. He knew he could not leave without doing something to help his father this final time.

A plan came to Baqash as he rode quickly away from Lemish's house to avoid being seen. He headed his megalosaur toward a guard post on the wall of the city where he knew he would find a few loyal men who would help him. When they reached the wall, Baqash called out to the warriors inside the guard house beside the wall's walkway. Several men ran out when they recognized the voice of their leader.

"It is Baqash!" one of the men cried as the group strode into the night. "I told you it was him." The men ran to the side of Baqash's megalosaur and gave him greetings. They were glad to see their true leader had returned.

"Baqash, what is this we hear that you will no longer be leading us?" asked another in the group, a desperate tone in his voice.

"There is not time for me to explain right now, so ask me no more questions. You will just have to trust me until I can tell you later. Right now I need a scouting party to go with me into the camp of the Damogans. This may be our only hope of defeating them before they overrun our city. Are any of you with me?

"I will always follow your lead, Baqash! You are the greatest leader we have," one of the men said boldly. All the other warriors agreed one by one, pledging their allegiance to follow his plan as well.

"Here is the plan then. We will leave the city by twos from all directions. Megado and I will go to the Damogan camp section where Boax is stationed near the enemy leader. We will find where they are sleeping and do away with them there. Each team will find the leader of his section and do away with him as well. Then we will all move behind the lines of the Damogans and shoot torched arrows into the air as soon as the earth has turned three degrees from where it is now. That should give us plenty of time. You, Kedmelen, go to my father's house and tell him to have the army ready to attack the Damogans as soon as they see the torches in the sky. With all their leaders dead, they will be confused and vulnerable to defeat. They will not be so quick to attack Cainogans again. It may be that Cainogan will be able to destroy the Damogans, add their territory to our province, and be free of their threats for good. Now get into your teams and move to your place of departure."

The men called out each other's names and went into the guard house to put on their weapons. As they scurried around, Megado asked Baqash, "Do you think your father will follow the plan?"

"We will know when the earth has moved three degrees," replied his master.

In that time nights and days were always clear. The water canopy did not allow clouds to hide the sun, moon, or stars. The men slipping out of the city and into the enemy camp would have to make their way through ravines and behind shrubs and crawl in the tall grass surrounding the city wall. Baqash and Megado would have to leave their megalosaurs behind and hope to confiscate other animals from the Damogans during the coming battle. They knew Boax and the Damogan leader would be camping in the area closest to the city's main gate. Boax would be there to protect the main body of leaders while they prepared to enter the city when the gates were opened to them.

The two warriors crawled through the grass, lying as low as they could. They knew the guards would not be expecting a surprise attack from the Cainogans at night. They felt sure that the Cainogans were trembling in fear behind their city walls, waiting to die. There had probably been a celebration and overuse of wine earlier in the evening, which would serve the stealthy warriors well.

When they crawled to the edge of the camp, there were few guards in sight. The one closest to them was half asleep. It did not take much effort for Megado to silence him with the right placement of his knife. Other warriors lay everywhere, asleep in bed rolls. Baqash and Megado looked for spears standing in the ground around a privacy tent. That would identify where the leader was bedded down, for he would have a privacy tent not afforded to the common warriors around him. Finally they saw the tent area on the far side of the campsite and moved toward it, being careful not to wake the sleeping warriors around them.

Just then a guard near the tent of the leader moved forward to get a better look at who was moving around in the camp. He did not want to yell for fear he would wake his leader unnecessarily. But he started toward them as Baqash grabbed a spear lying next to a warrior and threw it squarely into the guard's chest. The velocity of the spear knocked the guard backward as he fell dead on the ground.

Baqash moved quickly past the guard's body and glided into the leader's tent. A lamp was burning dimly inside, and Megado could see Baqash's shadow on the tent wall as he thrust his knife several times into a heap lying on a bed. The shadow then turned and left the tent. Baqash signaled for Megado to follow him as he moved around the side of the tent in a crouching walk.

"That is half our task finished," whispered Baqash as Megado caught up to him. "Now we must find Boax. It will give me much pleasure to cut his life short."

The two men looked over the many sleeping bodies lying everywhere, trying to detect the one that was more massive than the rest. Boax would not be far from the leader's tent. They listened for breathing that was much heavier than that of a normal man. Suddenly a huge shadow came from a clump of trees several yards from the tent where the two men were kneeling. It was Boax, who had gone into the woods to relieve himself. This was something they had not planned for. They did not have time to wait for the giant to lie down and go back to sleep.

Boax was huge, standing fourteen feet tall. He was not as heavy as Hercineolas, but he had well-defined muscles in his arms and legs and a neck as thick as a good-sized tree. He was agile and could move very quickly for a man his size. Now it seemed he had a sixth sense, for as he walked back to camp, he showed a concern that caused him to move toward the leader's tent with a hurried step. It was as though something told him the leader was in danger.

It was Megado who carried the bow and arrows, but he was not a skilled archer yet. He handed the bow and an arrow to Baqash, who had motioned to him for them, but his movement was pronounced enough for Boax to notice they were near the tent. The arrow of a normal man would not kill a Violent One unless it was aimed almost perfectly toward certain locations on his body. Baqash aimed and fired but missed his mark, wounding the hulk but not disabling him. Boax staggered for a second and pulled the arrow out of his upper chest. He made a move toward his weapons that lay beyond the tent, cursing and yelling as he passed them. Baqash gave a swipe of his sword at the back of the giant's knee as he ran by. The warriors in the camp were beginning to rouse from their slumber at the sound of the commotion Boax was making.

"Quick!" cried Baqash. "Go beyond the camp and fire a torched arrow!" Megado jumped to his feet, grabbed the bow, and ran as Baqash lunged to grab a spear that was stuck in the ground next to the tent. Boax was holding his leg and trying to get up at the same time. Baqash threw the spear into Boax's side, and the giant fell to the ground in agonizing pain. He was not dead, but he would be of no help to the Damogans in the battle tonight, and Baqash did not have time to finish him off. He could see that the warriors were going to be on him quickly, so he ran for the clump of trees where Megado had fled moments earlier. As he ran, he saw the torched arrow soar into the sky. He turned his head to see the other signal flares glowing in the night sky.

The Damogan warriors saw the signals as well, and it dawned on them that something was amiss. A cry of terror came from the tent, "He's dead! Our leader is dead!" All pursuit of the two infiltrators stopped as the confused warriors tried to make out what was happening in their camp.

Baqash and Megado climbed up a hill to see what would happen next. They could hear trumpet blasts, signaling for attack in the early morning darkness. The Cainogan forces had already been in place and were ready to attack the moment the flares went up. Cainogan had listened to Baqash's plan and followed through.

As the sound of battle raged below him, Baqash sat and wept bitterly over what had happened to him that night. He knew he could never again openly return to Madigan, for it would endanger his father's positions. He also knew he might never again see Landua. Lemish would see him as an enemy of Lucifer and never grant her to him. Landua would never be happy living a life on the run and would never have the opportunity to know Adoniel like Baqash had known him. From now on, Baqash would be a son dead to his family and all who knew him. He was now nothing more than a fugitive. But Baqash took heart in knowing he had helped his father overcome the Damogans, at least for now.

There was nothing left for Baqash or Megado in Cainogan

province. They would have to run for their very lives from the place they loved most, but even with all the hurt and pain that Baqash was feeling in this moment, he had a strange sense of newfound freedom, a freedom that called his heart to find the truth. He was free to begin his quest to find the garden, to see the tree, to read the creation story, to meet this man, Adam, the father of all human flesh. He was free to discover that for which Adoniel had died. If it took the rest of his life, Baqash was determined to live out his search for Eden. It might be that someday he would be able to return to his home so he could tell them of the truth he hoped to find.

Eight

The Quest Begins

The battle raged the rest of the night and into the early dawn. It was obvious that the Cainogans were routing the Damogans. They were weakened to the point that the Cainogans would be able to retaliate and take over the Damogan province as a part of their own. Baqash and Megado would not be there to help with the take-over, so instead they looked for a way to capture some new means of transportation to help them make their escape.

Two Damogan warriors rode up the hill where Baqash and Megado were hiding. The soldiers were trying to run before they were taken as captives, so Baqash and Megado positioned themselves behind trees in the path of the Damogans coming up the hill. At just the right moment, Baqash lunged from behind the tree and thrust his sword; Megado used his bow and a well-placed arrow to unseat the warriors from their mounts. The two Cainogans grabbed the reins of the two allosaurs and mounted quickly as the Damogans lay confused and wounded. In a full run, they headed northeast, leaving behind their home and the sounds of battle. They were on the road again, but they did not have to push the allosaurs as they had the megalosaurs. It was just as well because while the allosaurs were more spirited than megalosaurs, they were not quite as durable for long-distance runs.

Heading northeast Baqash and Megado knew they would pass through the Damogan province for several miles and would need to be careful about whom they met on the roads. It was especially necessary to be on the lookout for bands of traveling temple priests, who would be checking for the mark of the serpent on their wrists or foreheads. When Baqash and Megado went into cities or towns, they would need to be even more alert because people could receive a reward for turning in anyone who did not have the mark. There were also some professional bounty hunters who made a living bringing enemies of the serpent into the custody of the temple.

In order to plan their journey to the Four Forks in the River, the two travelers knew they must go to a large city beyond the Damogan province to find a house of maps. The closest large city would be Selch, in the Bandura province just east of Damogan. It was one hundred miles to the border of Bandura province, and Selch was another fifty miles beyond that. Going to this city was risky, for it was a city highly committed to the large temple standing in its midst. Lucifer worship was very strong. The men would have to try to get in unnoticed and get out as quickly as they could. They kept their allosaurs moving at a fast pace but did not push them too hard. They could reach the border by nightfall and camp overnight. They could then make Selch by midday on the morrow.

Evening was falling as the men rode into a clearing just off the road. It would make a good place to bed down for the night. Megado did all of the food gathering and preparation after he unsaddled and secured the animals. He had not forgotten that he was still a slave, and even though he was as much a fugitive as Baqash, nothing had changed in their relationship. They had been through a lot together, but Megado knew that he still had a master and that he was fortunate to have one who treated him with some respect.

After all the work was done, Baqash invited Megado to sit and talk with him awhile. He did not do this often, for he did not want Megado to forget his place. But this was a night Baqash felt a need to talk.

"Our lives have changed a lot in the last revolution round the sun," said Baqash, an air of contemplation about him.

"Yes, sir. Since we left Hellsrun, our lives will never be the same," Megado replied softly, almost to himself.

"Do you have regrets that I chose to reject the vows of Lucifer?" asked Baqash, wanting to learn how Megado really felt.

"Sir, it is not my place to have regrets. My only task is to obey the one I serve. You are the master; I am the slave. That is how it is. You are a great warrior. It is a privilege to serve a great warrior," Megado answered matter-of-factly. "But, yes. I have one regret, Master," he continued, as if a painful thought had come to mind. "I regret that night that I allowed us to be taken by surprise. I hope to one day regain your respect despite that show of weakness in the midst of my responsibility. I will one day redeem myself in your eyes."

"Every great warrior has something to prove to himself. It is sad that not all gain the opportunity. As enemies of Lucifer, I am sure you will get your chance to try to gain the redemption you seek. As for me, I feel I have lost all that I once lived for, yet something compels me to think there is far more for us to gain than what we have ever known in the past. There is truth out there waiting to be found, and I will find it. And when I do, I believe that all that has been lost to me I will find again." Baqash paused a moment and then spoke again. "I'll never forget the question Adoniel asked me as we traveled in his battle wagon: 'Who is the fool—the man who dies for living in the truth or the man who lives for accepting a lie?' I had no idea at the time that he was traveling to Hellsrun to live out his answer to that question before my very eyes. He was willing to die for the truth, the truth he lived for with all his being. That man knew things I have only dreamed about. I must see for myself those things that made Adoniel become the kind of man he was. Maybe those things can make me a man like him as well. If so, then all that is lost to me now will be nothing compared to what I will have found. If what he said is true, then I will be a man who can live in the truth, no longer living a lie."

"Well, Master, if that is your heart speaking, I hope we both find the redemption we seek," said Megado, deeply moved by what his master had just said. He realized Baqash had given him a trust he must not abuse, so he left his master alone with his thoughts as they both prepared to get some needed rest before the early morning light. They would need to leave early to make Selch by midday.

Selch was a city cut out of the midst of a beautiful forest, and it had many trees that caused it to blend into its surroundings. There were few tall buildings to rise above the city's encircling protective wall. The most distinct landmark in Selch was the temple that stood six stories high in the middle of the city. Smoke rose from the temple as priests led in the midday sacrifices. Most sacrifices were of animals and fruit from the ground that the people brought to be totally burned as a gift to Lucifer. The priests took much of the non-flesh gifts for their own food supply but there were times when a family offered a child sacrifice if they felt Lucifer had great anger against them. The smoke of the sacrifices rose through a smoke-stack that loomed high above the altar and was made in the image of a large cobra, reared in its striking position. All temples used this same pattern for their altars.

The province was at peace, so the gates of Selch were opened wide to allow the caravans and other travelers easy entry. Selch was at one of the crossroads of the world that allowed travelers to go east or west on trade routes or to go north and south to or from Hellsrun or other trade centers. For this reason, there was a very busy house of maps in the city. Thankfully, it was busy enough that two fugitives could use it and not be noticed.

Baqash and Megado tied their allosaurs outside the walls in a place where they felt they would be unnoticed for a short period of time. They then hid on the side of the road until a caravan came along. They had passed one on their way to Selch, so they knew it would be coming soon. As the caravan passed, they waited until a wagon came by that they could hide in until they entered the city. The large, slow-moving wagons had many places for hiding, and since the gates of cities were places where guards looked for the mark of Lucifer on those who entered, Baqash decided it would be best to sneak into the city rather than to ride in boldly.

The wagon the men were hiding in passed by the gate guard

without being checked, for the caravans were so long that random checks were only made unless a fugitive was known to be hiding there. Once it had traveled a short distance beyond the gate, Baqash jumped from the wagon. Megado followed suit when the way was clear. The two men then moved into the crowd of the bustling marketplace. It was a perfect place for strangers to go unnoticed.

Baqash and Megado followed the main street into the center of the city where they knew the map house would be, and they kept their eyes open for other travelers who looked like they might be going there as well. They soon spotted a group and followed them until the map house was in sight and entered a long, narrow, open-air hall with double-wide doors opened all the way around it. It had a roof, but it was not for protection from the weather. Buildings like these had to be locked at night to keep out thieves.

They entered the building and went to one of the many large map books lying side by side on a long table in the center of the hall. Mapmaking was a very important business in those times, for world travel was easily accessible. The worldwide religion of Lucifer, worldwide travel of caravans, and the constant battling of warlords also caused a great demand for the business of mapmaking. The people had learned from the ancient ones long ago that the world was round, and by this time men had developed a system of latitude and longitude to establish coordinates around the world. Men spent their lives recopying the maps and upgrading them, much like scribes recopied the holy book of Lucifer.

Baqash looked in the index for the coordinates of the Four Forks in the River. Megado stood by him, looking around to be sure no one tried to take them by surprise. Baqash found the coordinates to be forty-five degrees east longitude and thirty-five degrees north latitude. He then found the coordinates for Selch, which were ninety degrees west longitude and twenty degrees south latitude. Baqash turned the pages in the map book to find a description of the part of the earth that included the coordinates he had found. He learned that he would have to travel ten thousand miles north by northeast. They would journey north to the Equator Highway and then go east until they reached the Prime Meridian Sea. The Prime Meridian split the sea in half, giving the body of water its name. They would cross the sea in a northeast path that would bring them to the city of Krin and the Tropic of Cancer Highway. Next, they would follow the highway east until they passed the Gezing Mountains. Then they would move northeast following the Pishon River until they reached the land of the Four Forks in the River. They would pass through many cities, forests, and plains on the way. Though the map was old, the sea was charted fairly well and indicated the domains of leviathan sea monsters. This plan of travel would also avoid the known monasteries of the Violent Ones.

Baqash eyed the map for a good while until he had memorized the details. While he was concentrating on the map, Megado noticed a rough-looking man who was heavily armed with weapons, suggesting that he was a professional bounty hunter for the temple priests. As Megado watched him, he could see that his eyes wandered to other points, a clear indicator that he probably had some partners working with him.

Megado tried to act as though he did not notice the man was

stalking them. He spoke to Baqash without turning to look at him, "Master, there is a man who appears to be a bounty hunter watching us from across the street. It looks like he may have some men working to surround us."

"Continue to act as if we are unaware, Megado. We will exit the building opposite the opening we entered in. Once we reach the doorway, we will take off in separate directions and try to lose them in the marketplace crowd. Do not go straight back to the allosaurs, and before you do, be sure you have lost any pursuers. We will give ourselves two degrees to get back to the allosaurs, so check the position of the sun as we leave the building. If one of us is not back at the allosaurs within our time limit, the one who is free must make his escape alone. Leave the extra allosaur in case the other gets back late and can still get away. Do you understand?" Baqash tried to appear to be showing Megado the directions on the map as he outlined the escape plan.

Megado looked at the map as though he was receiving instruction on how to use it. By now the bounty hunter was moving slowly toward the map house. "Yes, sir, I understand fully. I hope to see you soon," he said as they moved toward the double-door exit that was across from their assailant.

As they came to the door, they could see another man moving toward them, so they bolted in opposite directions, heading into the crowded streets. The two bounty hunters separated as well and followed after the men. Baqash and Megado were at a disadvantage, for they did not know the city streets like those who were chasing them. Their biggest hope was to get out of sight long enough to find a place to hide and make the bounty hunters lose track of them.

Baqash ran down a side street, turned a corner, and ran until he could turn back toward the main street and the busy marketplace again. It was obvious that he was faster than his foe, for the man did not gain on him in his pursuit. As he rounded the corner, he had time to duck into a house of pleasure before he was seen by his follower. He stopped quickly and tried to enter without drawing attention to himself. Walking by a window, he saw the man run by without looking into the building. Baqash crossed the room to another exit and entered a side street going in the opposite direction of the bounty hunter. Now he could make his way to the allosaurs on the back streets that ran parallel to the main street. This would take him to the main gate area, but he would not leave through the gate and risk being seen again. The best thing to do would be to go over the city wall in a place where he would not be seen.

Guards' stairs led to the walkway on the city wall, allowing warriors to keep watch by looking over the wall. Baqash ran up the stairs, and when he reached the top, he waited until no one was watching, eased over to the wall, crawled up and over it, and dropped about twenty feet to the ground. He then made his way back to the allosaurs.

The allosaurs were still where they had been tied, and there was no sign that anyone had tampered with them. But where was Megado? It was almost rendezvous time—the earth had almost moved the allotted two degrees. Questions filled Baqash's mind, and he became impatient. "Where is he? Did he get caught? Is he lost? Is he still hiding? It is time to leave. Should I wait or go? I'll wait a little longer. Why hasn't' he come?" Baqash untied the allosaurs and moved them into the thicket to wait a little longer, hoping that Megado would make it back.

Baqash finally felt that he could stay no longer. He knew the bounty hunter would go and get help from the temple priests, and they would give him guards to make a search for them all over the city area, inside and outside the city wall. He led his allosaur into the clearing, intending to mount and run, but he was having great difficulty forcing himself to do what he least wanted. In frustration he put his foot into the stirrup and began to pull himself up into the saddle.

Just then a figure of a man slid into the clearing. He was out of breath and exuded an odor that made the allosaur recoil. He was filthy from head to foot. "Master! Master!" he cried in great excitement. "You are still here!" It was Megado.

Baqash jumped down from his mount and hurried over to make sure Megado was all right. He had not realized how much the slave had come to mean to him until now. He picked him up from the ground and asked excitedly, "Where have you been? I almost left you behind! What is that terrible smell?"

"Oh, Master, I ran as fast as I could to escape the man who chased me. I finally saw a row of wagons lined up on the side of a street, so I jumped into one, hoping the man would run by and not see me. I did not know the wagons were full of dried animal dung to be taken to the fields for fertilizer. When I got in the wagon, the field workers came and moved the wagons. I could not get out until they left the gates on the other side of the city. I had to run all the way around the city wall to get here, just to stay out of sight. I was afraid you were already gone."

"Well, get on your allosaur if it will let you. Let's get out of here. You can clean up in a river somewhere down the road." Baqash tried to be stern with his slave, but the mixture of relief at seeing Megado again and the humorous sight of his filthy slave made it impossible. Finally he broke into laughter as they mounted and rode away into the woods, away from Selch. They had evaded the bounty hunters—at least for now. But there were many ruthless bounty hunters in the world, and they probably had not seen the last of their kind.

Nine

The Prime Meridian Sea

Baqash and Megado finally arrived at the Equatorial Highway, the most-traveled east-west highway in the world because it was at the very center of the earth and divided the northern and southern hemispheres. Many great cities lay along the path of the highway. In addition there were three major seas that lay on the equator; the highway traveled around them. It was also possible to catch a sea barge that carried travelers across the water to reach the highway on the other side.

But there was one huge problem for sea travelers: the great leviathan population was growing all over the world, making it harder and harder for sea travel to be profitable. These large, dragon-like animals were almost impossible to kill or tame, and they were very protective of their domains. At maturity, each male established his own domain in a sea. It was hard to determine where new domains were established unless a sea barge was attacked and survivors were able to tell about it. Something needed to be done about this growing menace, but for now the leviathans had to be tolerated.

Baqash had an idea that might help him and Megado in their travels, making them less conspicuous to those looking for unmarked temple rebels. In the next city they would try to enlist as guards for a caravan traveling east and west. Often the caravan masters were more concerned about business than religion and did not ask many questions. Usually the warrior guards of these caravans were running from something, but if they were good fighters who could hold their own against bandits, that was usually all the caravan master cared about.

Baqash proposed that he and Megado could pose as Damogan warriors who had fled from the Cainogan war. That way there would be no question as to why they were riding allosaurs with Damogan trappings. It would also keep suspicion away from them if priests came looking for two Cainogans who had fled from Hellsrun without taking their vows of submission and receiving their marks. It seemed like a good plan. Attaching themselves to a caravan would cause them to travel much more slowly, but they were not in a hurry as they had been when they made their trip to Hellsrun and back. They could go in and out of cities with the caravan and avoid being checked for the mark as often as they would be if traveling alone.

The first large city they would come to on the Equatorial Highway was Baaloda. It was the third largest city in the world and a perfect place to remain unnoticed until they could find a caravan master to hook up with. Until then they would just have to take their chances at not being discovered.

The broad highway led right through the middle of the metropolis of Baaloda. There were no guards checking for marks, for there was too much traffic coming and going, and it would take an army to check everyone. Traffic would be backed up for miles, and it would take travelers and caravans days just to get in and out of the city. That would be bad for business, and business was the priority at Baaloda.

The two men headed straight for the business district of the city where the caravans loaded and unloaded their goods. There the caravans also paid their road use taxes and bought their trading licenses to do business in the city. They did all their unloading in this district and then transferred the goods they hoped to sell to the several marketplaces around the city.

Baqash decided to wait until evening to talk to a caravan master at a house of pleasure close to the caravan corrals. The caravan workers would be in these places after a long journey, seeking the food, drink, and entertainment these places provided. By then, anyone they talked to would be in a better mood and more approachable than during a busy day of work.

There was one place of business that night that seemed louder than the others around it. It was probably the best choice to try first at finding a caravan master. Baqash and Megado walked in slowly so as to not draw attention to themselves. Their plan was to go in, look the place over, and then wait for the right time to introduce themselves to a master.

The place was full of smoke from the weed pipes almost everyone was smoking. Many patrons were loud and boisterous as they drank their wine and barley beer and watched an "anything goes" fighting match in the center of the room where a professional fighter who was taking on anyone who was willing to test his fighting skills. Most men were braver now that they were drunk than they would have been sober, but still the professional was not being tested much. Those who placed wagers against him were making bad bets.

Baqash noticed a rather large and expensively dressed man at a table next to the fighting arena. He was laughing loudly, and many sought his attention as they sat nearby. He certainly looked like a rich caravan master. Baqash talked to the servant who brought them some food and drink and asked who the rich man was.

"That is Raglous," the servant answered. "He owns several caravans. He has many wives, and his sons work the other caravans for him. The fighter works for him, too. He will pay two hundred gold coins to anyone who can beat his man. You have to pay him one gold coin to fight."

Baqash sized up the fighter. He watched his fighting technique to determine any weaknesses he might have. The fighter was bigger and stronger than most men and could knock out a man with the right punch because he knew just where to strike. As Baqash watched him, he noticed the man set up his opponent with jabs from his left fist and then a cross from his right fist. After several of these combinations, he would then use a right upper cut as his opponent tried to parry the right cross he was expecting. The unsuspecting challenger was then wide open for a heavy blow to the chin. Of course the trained fighter then directed several blows to his opponent's body to wear him down. Often a man was so drunk that a few blows to the ribs were enough to finish him.

Baqash had learned the art of fighting as part of his warrior training, and he saw a match with the professional as his opportunity to get the caravan master's attention. If he could beat the man, he might win Raglous's respect—enough to earn himself and Megado jobs guarding his caravan. Baqash waited until two more men were finished off and then walked into the arena to make his challenge.

There was a lull in the noise as the champion was allowed a time to rest. Baqash walked up to the man taking the money and gave him a gold coin.

"What is your name?" asked the money taker.

"I am Benomi of the Damogans," replied Baqash, showing confidence as he pulled off his leather vest. He left his gloves on so no one would see that he had no mark on his wrists. His brown hair reached down the back of his neck to the top of his shoulders. As he turned to face the champion fighter, the lamplight showed Baqash was much thinner than the professional and not as tall. The fighter was big and burly while Baqash was thin and well-defined. Everyone placed their bets on the champion.

The money taker came to the middle of the ring and announced the challenger, "The next opponent is Benomi, the Damogan warrior."

Megado grinned at the thought of his master being called a Damogan warrior. There was not much response from the crowd except for a few boos from those who didn't look forward to another boring fight from a lesser opponent than the champion. The rules were simple: fight until just one man was standing.

Suddenly the champion came at Baqash. He apparently thought he would finish this skinny runt quickly. Baqash knew he could not give away his abilities too soon. It would be better if his opponent did not take him seriously. He knew he would have to take a few punches to make the fighter overconfident enough to become careless.

Baqash tried to look clumsy at first as he moved around and allowed himself to be hit, but not with any direct blows. He knew a solid blow from this massive man would leave him lying on the floor, senseless, so he was careful not to take any direct hits. He tried to act as though the blows that did hit him were hurting him, and some really did. Baqash waited for the man to go into his knockout sequence, hoping to maintain his strength until the right moment when he could land a hard enough blow to take out this brute. He might not get another chance if he missed on his first try.

Baqash's strategy was working. The champion was preparing to make his move on Baqash, thinking he had the upper hand against this seemingly novice fighter. He began his sequence of left jabs and right crosses. The key for Baqash was to anticipate the right upper cut and strike first. He kept his eyes on the champion, watching for any slight evidence that the fighter was ready to make his move. Suddenly Baqash saw it. Just as his opponent made his second left jab, the man slightly dropped his right fist instead of raising it. When Baqash saw that drop, he immediately stepped to his own left, away from the coming right upper cut. As he stepped, he landed a strong left jab directly to the jaw of his foe. The blow stunned the man just long enough for Baqash to land a crushing upper cut to his chin and then come back with a finishing left blow to the side of the champion's head. The huge man did not look like he was quite finished, so Baqash brought his knee straight up into the weakened man's gut, causing him to bend over. He struck a final blow to the ex-champion's jaw, causing him to fall like a tree, flat on his back. He lay there for several minutes and did not move.

The crowd yelled at the limp hulk, trying to make him get up, but their cries fell on clouded, confused, dizzy ears. It would be a while before this fallen hero would rise again. Baqash stood watching in the ready position, just in case the fighter wasn't finished. Finally he turned and walked toward Raglous. When he looked the caravan master in the eye, Baqash could see that he was genuinely impressed.

Baqash stood without a word until the man spoke. "Well, I guess I owe you two hundred gold pieces, Damogan warrior. I have never known the Damogans to be great fighters, but I guess you have given me reason to change my opinion. That was quite a skilled piece of work you exhibited out there."

"Sometimes a man's greatest asset can be another man's wrong impression," said Baqash, matter-of- factly. "When your fighter wakes up, you might tell him to take nothing for granted until the battle is won."

"I will send my man to get you your money."

"It is not your money I desire, sir. I have been told that you are the great Raglous, and I wanted to win this fight tonight to show you that I can be a capable guard in your service. It would be a great honor for me and my slave over there to protect you and your goods as you travel in this thief-ridden world."

"Well, now, that is a great proposition. I must trade my great fighter for a guard on my caravan." Raglous laughed as his whole body shook. Regaining his composure, he continued, "I will make you a deal, Damogan warrior. I will let you and your slave serve me if you will agree to stay away from my champion fighter. He has made me too much money to give up on him now. I am sure he will fight better after his lesson tonight." The man laughed again as the professional fighter began to come around in the middle of the arena floor. "Follow my man over there, and he will show you where the guards have taken rooms for the night."

Baqash motioned for Megado to follow as he moved over to meet Raglous's slave. The slave turned and walked out of the house of pleasure as Baqash followed and Megado hurried across the room to catch up. They had achieved their goal of employment but had made an enemy of the fighter—and of some who had lost their sure bets. For now, however, they could take advantage of their new cover-up.

The next day, the head guard found Baqash and explained to him what his duties would be. He and Megado would be part of the rear guard that followed the caravan. That was where all the newcomers were placed until they proved themselves to be worthy enough to move up toward the front. Raglous also knew that his fighter would not see Baqash much there, and that would keep to a minimum the possibility of tension growing between the two. That was fine with Baqash. He did not want to face the fighter again, for he might have changed his technique for the better.

The caravan had already been doing business in Baaloda for several rotations. The two new guards made trips back and forth from the marketplace to the caravan station, guarding the unsold goods that were to be packed and moved to the next city of trade. The two men were unnoticed and accepted as part of the caravan company. People kept their distance from Baqash out of respect for his total domination over the fighter.

It took two rotations to get the caravan ready, but finally the journey began, heading east. It was slow moving along the highway. The caravan was about a mile long, and it would be several rotations before they arrived at the next city, where they would stop for a long period of time. The guards at the rear kept a lookout for any suspicious developments, such as faster moving groups coming from behind. They also kept watch for any possible surprise attacks that could come out of the forests on either side of the highway. They stayed alert for signs from the flank guards and front guards that would call for back-up in case of attack from those positions. The guards were also responsible for helping fix any breakdowns and staying behind with any groups in the caravan that might have to take a lot of time to be repaired. When that happened, the caravan would move on, and those left behind would catch up later.

As they traveled down the highway, Baqash often thought of home and Landua. He remembered those days growing up in Madigan when his sister was still home and he was training as a young warrior. Those were days of great expectation and excitement about future possibilities. It was amazing to him that his life now was so removed from what he had looked forward to. But those thoughts and memories were displaced by a hunger in his heart to satisfy, once and for all, that inward need for deliverance from bondage to a life controlled by a serpent god religion he could not accept. Hope was growing in his heart that what he would find at the Four Forks in the River would answer all the nagging questions in his inner being. The thought of finding that kind of peace helped ease the hurt of his lost dreams.

The trip from Baaloda to the Prime Meridian Sea would take several months, and they stopped in four large cities on the way. Baqash planned to leave the caravan when they got to the sea. The caravan would travel south around the sea to stop in cities on the coast along the highway, but Baqash and Megado would catch a sea barge and move northeast to a city close to the Tropic of Cancer Highway. By then they would have made enough money to pay their way to their destination.

The trip was fairly uneventful. Baqash stayed away from the fighter, who continued to make good money for Raglous. He had changed his fighting style a little, trying not to be as predictable with his punches as before.

The temple priests in the cities did not bother Raglous's caravans. He brought too many of the goods they wanted. He also paid a lot of tax money into the cities and put quite a bit into the temple treasury in order to be left alone. Baqash and Megado just did their jobs and tried to remain as anonymous as possible.

Meditrainia was a beautiful city on the coast of the Prime Meridian Sea. It was one of those cities in which everyone wanted to spend a holiday when it was safe enough to travel. There were also several rivers that emptied into the sea at that point, which made commerce very strong. The caravan would stay here longer than most places, for it was the halfway point in their journey around the globe.

Ten

A Trip on a Sea Barge

After the caravan got settled in and the goods had been moved to the markets for sale, Baqash had some free time to go to the pier and find a sea barge on which to book a passage for himself, Megado, and their allosaurs. He talked to several barge masters and found they were unwilling to make the trip across the sea because it had become too dangerous. The leviathans were growing in number, and some of their new domains were uncharted. Fewer and fewer travelers were willing to travel by sea, for word had gotten out that it was too dangerous. Those sea barge masters willing to make the trip could not do so because it was not profitable. They had to wait several weeks to obtain enough cargo and passengers to make a trip worthwhile. Then once they got across the sea, they had no guarantee of being able to return.

The sun had moved several degrees across the sky when Baqash came across an old barge that had a sign saying, "Desperate—must make one more crossing to Krin." Baqash remembered that Krin was the city on the map where he wanted to land so that he could continue his journey to the Tropic of Cancer Highway.

Baqash walked onto the barge to see if he could find the master.

There was not a lot of activity going on. In fact, there was no activity at all. The sea barge had three stories. The first was a main deck for cargo and animals. It was long and wide and low to the water. The next story was for lighter cargo and the passengers' luggage. The top story contained quarters for the passengers. The captain directed the ship at the top of the barge, above the passengers.

As was typical of sea vessels in those days, the barge was powered by a conveyor belt in the middle that was attached to paddle wheels in the center of each side of the ship. Different teams of animals could be used to walk on the conveyor belt to power the paddle wheels, such as mammoths, triceratops, elephants, rhinoceroses, and horses. Smaller barges could use one or two animals instead of a whole team.

Baqash finally heard some movement on the second deck where the lighter cargo was stored. He walked up the stairs and made his way toward the mysterious noise. As he got closer, he heard a voice grumbling, cursing, and complaining about his misfortune for the lack of cargo and passengers and for the help he could not afford.

Baqash turned a corner around a stack of bundles. There, bent over a fairly large package, was a balding, gray-haired man, struggling to stack a piece of cargo on top of some crates. In times past, Baqash would not have felt a responsibility to help the old man, but something compelled him now to reach down, grab the load, and lift it alongside the frustrated sea barge master. The old man was startled to have his load lightened a bit but continued to lift until the package was in place.

"Whew! That was a heavy one, young warrior," said the barge master, stretching his back and arms. "My name is Bodand. You lookin' for a ride across the sea?"

"My slave and I are ready to make the trip as soon as possible. What is the fare?"

"It will be awhile before I can be ready to shove off. I want to have enough cargo and passengers to make it worth my while, and this will be my last trip. I'm getting out of the business when I get back to Krin. It's gotten too dangerous. I can't make a living; not many are willing to make the trip anymore. The leviathans are getting harder and harder to avoid. Do you have a name, warrior?"

"My name is of no interest to you, sir. What's your fare?" asked Baqash a second time.

"Oh, one of those, huh? Well, I always have to charge more for those who don't have a name. I never know what kind of trouble I might be bringing on myself, carrying anonymous passengers. Not that I won't take you, mind you, but I have to be careful. I'll have to charge you thirty dandrii each—that is, unless you want to work for part of your fare. I'll need a hand with keeping the team of horses fed and moving. That would only cost you fifteen dandrii each."

"How soon will you be ready to leave?" asked Baqash.

"I have very little cargo and no passengers right now. I plan to leave in fourteen rotations regardless of what has come my way. I cannot stay here for the rest of my time."

"I will be back at that time with my slave, and we will help you make your trip for fifteen dandrii each." Baqash turned and walked away, making his way off the sea barge. He went back to the caravan station to work and wait for the departure time. The caravan would stay in Meditrainia at least that long.

The time went by quickly. Baqash had become accustomed to the work, and it had turned out to be a perfect cover for Megado and him. They were overlooked by the temple priests in every town they entered. Raglous apparently had put the word out to leave them alone. Baqash did not feel good about leaving Raglous. He had become a friend and had paid well for the work they had done, but it was time to move on with their quest to find the place called Eden.

It seemed risky to be taking the sea route instead of staying with the caravan. The leviathan threat was a very real possibility, but Baqash had determined that it was not wise to stay in one situation too long. The longer he stayed, the greater the possibility grew that they would be discovered. He was willing to risk the leviathans rather than stay any longer with the caravan.

Baqash did not say anything to Raglous about leaving. He wanted to avoid leaving behind any trails for bounty hunters or priests to track. He felt it would be better to just disappear without a trace. He and Megado waited until late in the night, when the men around them had drunk themselves to sleep after spending time at a pleasure house, wagering on the fights there. They left in the opposite direction of the piers in case someone saw them leave. Later they made their way back around to the dock where they would embark with Bodand for Krin.

By the looks of the sea barge when they arrived, Bodand had not loaded a lot more cargo. Apparently not much had changed;

sea travel was still not popular. Baqash wondered if Bodand would still be willing to make the trip.

The sun began to radiate the wonderful pink hue in the horizon of the early morning sunrise as the two men led their allosaurs onto the sea barge. They read the sign that was still on display as they left the pier: "Desperate—must make one more crossing to Krin."

They could hear movement on the upper deck as they tied the animals to a pen post next to the pen where the team of six horses that powered the barge was kept. They heard Bodand coming as he called out to what he hoped would be new customers, "Hello! I'll be right there. Glad to have you aboard." His look of excitement changed to disappointment when he saw who it was. These were not full-paying customers. But then he perked up again as he remembered he would at least not have to make this last trip to Krin alone. "Well, you came back, did you? I wondered if you might have a change of heart when you had some time to think about the trip. Well, I'm glad you're back, and the offer is still good if you want to take it."

"We are ready to get started when you say the word, sir," said Baqash, his voice guarded. He did not yet know if this was a man he could trust. He would keep him at arm's length until he had a better feel for the man's true character. He handed the master fifteen dandrii and said, "Here is half our payment now. I will pay the rest when we arrive at Krin."

"It is the accepted way, said Bodand as he put the money in his pouch. "Why don't you and your slave there get the horses hitched up to the power track? I'll get ready to shove off. You be ready to untie us from the pier when I give the word."

Baqash and Megado worked together to harness the six horses. It was a regular wagon harness that hitched the horses in a two-by-two line and then coupled them to rails on each side of the power track treadmill in the middle of the barge. As they finished clipping the harness to the side rails, Bodand yelled, "Turn us loose!" He began to ring a bell as his two helpers pulled the huge ropes free from the pier. The bell was pointless, for there were no other barges leaving that day or any day soon, which made the empty exit canal feel strangely eerie. Megado grabbed the reins to the team of horses and got them moving as Bodand guided the barge out into the clear.

The three men had the sea barge all to themselves. There were no other travelers willing to take the risk with them, but the three-day trip would not take a lot of work on any one man's part. They fed the animals from feed bags and ate meals of prepared bread, fresh fruits, eggs, and vegetables. Bodand taught them to steer the barge by keeping a right angle with the magnetic needle that pointed due north and was mounted in front of the steering wheel. The wheel controlled the rudder at the back of the barge, and each man took his turn at it.

The water was calm as the barge moved forward. Occasionally the travelers saw a school of flying fish sailing out of the water, and several porpoises escorted the barge for awhile. In the distance a whale blew from the water, splashed down in a crash of waves, and dove as its huge tail fin made a final push back into the depths of the sea. At times the long neck of a plesiosaur jutted from the water as it came forging by. The active sea life was a good sign that the dreaded leviathan was not in these waters.

That evening as Megado took his turn at the wheel, Bodand and Baqash ate their meal together. There were questions that Baqash wanted to ask Bodand, so he took a seat at the table with the sea barge master. They enjoyed a meal of bread, eggs, vegetables, and fruit.

"What are the chances that we will encounter a leviathan?" asked Baqash.

"That is hard to know," replied Bodand. "The population has increased, and there have been more sightings than ever before. There have also been more cases of barges not arriving at their destinations. I am on a course that so far has been free of any hazards since it has been traveled."

"Have you ever seen a leviathan in your travels?"

"Only once, several rotations ago. I hope to never see another. We escaped destruction only because another leviathan came along and challenged our assailant for his territorial domain. Leviathan will attack any living or non-living thing that it perceives is a threat to its domain. We eased away as the two tore into each other. The fury of their battle was so great that the waves they caused almost overturned our small barge. I learned from that encounter to only travel the most recently charted waters."

"What does a leviathan look like? What should we expect if one attacks us? Is there no weakness they have that can be exploited?"

"Leviathan, from the tip of its nose to the tip of its tail, is as long as the largest whale. It has a head bigger than a behemoth, with a longer snout and many more teeth. Its head is supported by a thick, powerful neck half the length of a plesiosaur. It swims like a crocodile with its long, broad tail and can grasp with the talons of a giant eagle on his webbed front and hind feet. Those feet extend from large, powerful legs. It breathes fire and smoke and has a roar that turns the bravest of men to stone. It is covered with thick scales that no arrow or spear can pierce, and they are so close together that no wound can be made between them. Expect this fierce fighter to be relentless. Whatever it battles, it does so to the death. That is why vessels that are attacked never survive. The leviathan does not think it has conquered until the barge is sinking." As Bodand spoke, his eyes revealed a fear that Baqash had never before seen in a man. He knew this man was telling no tales; he spoke from experience."

"Why do you make this final trip to Krin and take the chance of a possible attack from such a creature? Why did you not sell the barge in Meditrainia and catch a wagon that would circle round the sea as all others are doing these days?"

"You are a man full of questions, yet you give so few answers yourself," replied Bodand, looking Baqash in the eye. "This barge is all I've known for the last fifty revolutions of my life. It is all I have. Krin is my home, but without my barge, I would have nothing when I got there. No one today is looking to buy a barge, let alone willing to pay a top price. In Krin I can wait this out and start over when sea travel becomes profitable again. I can travel the coast and up some of the rivers and make a pretty good living. I figure this route I'm taking ought to be safe for at least this last trip."

During the late night hours it was Baqash who stood at the

wheel, holding the barge on course. The stars were aglow as always, and Baqash had fixed the front tip of the barge on one of them, straight on line with his course. He daydreamed about his life back in Cainogan, remembering the times he had spent with Landua. It seemed like ages ago now.

Without warning, there was a surge to the right of the vessel that came with such force it almost overturned. The fact that Baqash held onto the wheel was the only reason he was not slammed into the wall of the wheel house. As the barge stabilized, there came a roar so fierce it made his ears ring. He could hear the horses shrieking in fear as they fell over themselves, constrained by the bonds of their harnesses. The paddle wheels had stopped moving as the horses lay kicking in confusion on the power track, unable to regain their standing position.

Baqash crawled from the wheel house just in time to see the webbed talons of a huge reptile paw crash down on the side of the barge, making it lurch once again. As Baqash looked up and the barge dipped to its side like a toy, he found himself looking straight into the eye of the most fierce looking creature he had ever seen. Rolling to his left down the rail, he avoided being scorched by flame as it bellowed out of a mouth large enough to break one of the horses in two with one crushing bite. The beast gave another deafening roar as the barge popped back up out of the water, trying to right itself.

Baqash jumped from the top deck to the passenger deck below. He ran into the eating quarters where he found Megado lying on the floor next to the wall. Tables and chairs had rolled over on him, and he was out cold. Baqash pulled the furniture from Megado, hoisted him over his shoulder, and ran to the other side of the room as the barge began to lean in that direction. Tables and chairs slammed around him as he carried Megado out the doorway on the opposite side from where the leviathan was attacking the barge. *Where is Bodand?* he wondered as he heard the monster tear the other side of the upper deck from the barge in a fierce, escalating rage.

Baqash had to do something fast, knowing it would not be long before the barge would break up. He remembered what Bodand had said: Leviathans fight to the death. He knew his only hope was to shove some floating objects off the barge while the sea monster fought to destroy it. Perhaps they could float on the debris in the open sea and try to make it to land.

Now the monster had turned away from the barge and was using its huge tail to land heavy, vicious blows across the front. Each strike caused the whole vessel to sink and then rebound high out of the water. Baqash regained his footing each time, just enough to throw whatever he could into the sea before the tail smashed the barge again. He kept looking around in hopes of seeing Bodand. The horses were hopelessly thrashing their legs as they lay tangled together between the power track rails. *Where is Bodand?* he thought in great frustration.

Suddenly it became dangerously quiet as the barge bobbed in the churning water. The leviathan had vanished underwater. Before he could catch his breath, Baqash realized what was about to happen. He picked up Megado, threw him into the sea, and jumped in after him. Just as Baqash hit the water, the barge leaped from the waves as the force of the gigantic animal crashed into the hull of the barge, causing it to completely lift out of the water and then overturn. Falling into the sea, the barge began to break apart. Baqash grabbed Megado and pulled him to safety as the leviathan thrashed and roared, relentlessly discharging huge gusts of flame at the helpless hulk in the water. It continued to tear at the remains of the vessel with its talons, ripping and tossing huge chunks of the wooden craft into the air. The beast would not be appeased until its foe was totally ripped apart.

Baqash was finally able to grab some of the debris floating in the water. He caught hold of a piece of cargo large enough to carry Megado and pushed him onto the floating box. He held onto the side of the makeshift, one-man raft as he continued to be tossed in the waves from the wake of the leviathan, still battling the barge now a safe distance away.

As he watched the animal finish off the sea barge, Baqash was amazed at the size and ferocity of this giant dragon. He thought, *Surely Bodand made no exaggeration; this truly is the most vicious animal in all the world.* Then he remembered what he had seen in battle—the merciless pride he had felt in his own heart standing over a dead foe, the bloodthirsty murders in the arena at Hellsrun, and the meaningless sacrifices of helpless women and baby girls in the temples of the serpent—and he had a change of heart. *No, this animal is only trying to protect its domain. Man kills for the lust of killing. Man is more vicious than any of the animals.*

Baqash bobbed in the open sea, clinging to a plank of wood and staring into the dark night. He was amazed he was still alive and wondered what he would have to face next.

Eleven

The Captives

There were a lot of broken remains of the barge floating around in the water. The leviathan had given his final roar of triumph and disappeared into the depths long ago. Baqash had managed to salvage some rope to tie several boxes together to make a small raft. He had also collected some pieces of wood that could be used as oars to paddle the raft toward land. He and Megado would use the sun by day and the stars by night to guide them in paddling due east. Land had to be at least several rotations of the earth away.

Megado had finally revived after a long period of unconsciousness. He remembered nothing of the attack except being awakened by a fierce roar. He had tried to run from his quarters to the wheel house through the eating area, but when the barge leaned hard, he was thrown into the wall. Apparently a table struck him in the head as he hit the wall. He woke up and found himself floating on a raft with a dull, throbbing headache.

They were able to keep their strength by eating plankton and drinking the sea water. In those days, the sea water was not salty, and they could survive for quite some time because the canopy over the earth protected them from severe heat and sunburn. There were no predatory animals at that time, so they did not fear attack from the large fish, sea mammals, and reptiles they occasionally spotted. Their only real concern was another possible encounter with a leviathan. They hoped their little raft would not be seen as a threat to another's domain.

The two men sat on their knees at the edge of the raft and kept the raft moving east as best they could. They talked awhile and then had long periods of silence. Megado broke one of those times of silence with a question. "Master, do you think Bodand survived the attack?"

"No, I think he was so emotionally tied to the barge that he would not have tried to leave it. I wish I could have gotten to know the man better. I think he was someone who would have protected our secret. He did not ask a lot of questions, which tells me he was satisfied not to know until we offered to tell him. It really is too bad we did not get to know him better. He would have been a good friend."

"Master, do you sense that there is a force or some kind of power bigger than we are that is somehow protecting us? We have been through so much, yet we still survive. Maybe there is a good kind of God like Dago told me about on the war wagon."

"Well, if there is a God protecting us, I sure would like to have a lot more protection and a lot less deliverance from these ordeals! I wonder about a God who protects a great warrior like Adoniel the way He did. I cannot say I am ready to believe in this God yet, but I must say I have felt some things in these days since I met Adoniel that I have never felt before."

"Master, do you think it may be that Adoniel did what he was supposed to do and really had more victory in dying than he would have in living? I have never seen and felt power in my life like the day I saw that man die. It was as if he was the real winner, and everyone in that arena knew it."

"I will agree something was there that I had not known before. I guess that is why I must find that garden he told me about. It is as if I will find the reason for his power when I see that place for myself. I will not fully believe until I can see for myself this place called Eden."

"Master, you have lost so much in all that has happened, but I feel I have gained everything. Though I am still a slave, there is something in me that tells me I am free. My freedom came when I chose to believe. It no longer matters to me if I see this place called Eden. Though I have not seen Eden, I have seen what its Creator has done to men like Dago and Adoniel, and what I see in them makes me believe."

"I wish it were that simple for me, but then I am not a slave, and I need something more than your emotions. Garden or no garden, my life will never be the same. Had I not met Adoniel, we would probably have marks on our wrists and still be in Cainogan." Baqash paused in mounting frustration. Then he continued angrily, "I do not want to talk about it, and do not bring up the subject again. You need to remember one thing as well: you are a slave, and you will be wise to not forget that. Do you understand?"

"Yes, Master, I understand," Megado replied humbly. He kept rowing, not offended by his master's harsh words. He knew what he felt, and that was enough for him. Baqash also rowed, sensing that same kind of calm power he had seen in Adoniel growing in his slave, Megado. It made him uneasy. It was something he could not control.

The two men rowed all during the hours of light and into the darkness. They then began to see a shadow rising in the starlit dark, along the eastern horizon. The closer they got to the shadow, the more distinct it became. It was a mysterious island, standing in the midst of the sea. It seemed to be very large, covering several square miles. It was mysterious because Baqash did not remember having seen the island on the map in Selch. An island this large should have been included. Why wasn't it on the map? Baqash asked himself.

As they drew closer to the beach, the roar of waves upon the shore grew louder and louder. There was something eerie about this island that caused Baqash and Megado to not get too excited about finding a refuge from the sea. Maybe they had been through so much that they had learned not to think too positively about a situation until they knew what lay in store for them. Maybe they were exhausted from rowing with clumsy makeshift oars for such a long time. Maybe something was telling them that they should be very cautious. For whatever reason, they got off the clumsy raft when they reached shallow water and pulled it up on the beach, being careful to look around them for any possible surprises.

The sandy white beach was narrowed by the high tide of the full moon. There was a dense forest that rose like a tall, foreboding wall just a few yards from the water, and the two men took some time to hide their makeshift raft in the thick brush, sweeping away the tracks in the sand with tree limbs. They did not want to give themselves away to any possible enemy that might inhabit the island. They found a place to hide themselves in a clump of bushes and took a little time to get some much-needed sleep before starting their expedition to explore this mysterious place.

It had been light for a good while when the two men began their new adventure. Moving with caution, they looked for any signs of human habitation. They hoped to climb to a high spot that would allow them to see more of the island at one time. For the most part, they found it to be fairly flat and covered by a thick forest.

They moved deeper and deeper into the jungle, seeing animal life of all kinds. Monkeys scrambled in the trees as the men passed beneath them, and birds gave a variety of calls. Snakes and insects crawled, and occasionally the roar of a large cat echoed through the trees. At one point they saw a group of brontosauruses reaching their long necks toward leaves high in the trees. There was a lot of wildlife on the island, but they saw no sign of humans.

Baqash and Megado made slow progress through the thick brush without a sword to help cut a path, but they were determined to know the island well before they could feel safe about being there. Suddenly and without warning they found themselves in a large clearing, looking at a very tall wall that was built around a large village of some sort. There was no activity outside the wall. However, there was indeed life of some kind on the other side, for sounds of clashing steel and grunts and groans of struggling men could be heard from beyond the wall. Baqash and Megado stayed in the brush at the edge of the clearing, not wanting to be discovered by those inside the enclosure. They also did not want to rush into the village until they had some idea who lived there.

The wall was no taller than the trees that surrounded the open space, so Baqash began to climb a giant redwood that was tall enough to let him see over the wall. It took quite some time to get to the top, and he did not like what he saw when he got there.

This was not a village; it was a fortress. Baqash found himself looking into a training village for Violent Ones. The sounds they heard were young Violent Ones, training in sword fighting and hand-to-hand combat. Temple priests were everywhere, and there were several behemoths in pens, apparently being trained to be killers. This was the last place men like Baqash and Megado needed to be.

No wonder this island was not on the map, thought Baqash as he made his way down the tree. *This is a secret training fortress. The priests of Lucifer have used their influence to keep the island off the map and have caused sea travel to be routed away from it. If we are caught here, we will never escape alive. This is double trouble. We do not have the mark of the serpent, and now we know where a secret training fortress is. If there is a good God out there protecting us, this is some backward way of doing it.*

Baqash continued to lower himself carefully by holding on to large chunks of bark. He then jumped the final ten feet to the ground. To Megado he said, "You had better ask the God of Adoniel to do something on our behalf, Megado. It seems we have stumbled upon a stronghold of Lucifer himself. This is a training fortress for Violent Ones. We must get off this island as soon as possible. I'm sure they patrol the island heavily. We cannot allow ourselves to be seen. There must be a supply harbor somewhere on the shore of the island where they load and unload sea barges from the mainland. We will secretly board one of those barges, hide in the cargo hold, and let it take us to the mainland. That is our best chance of escape."

The two men stayed among the trees as they moved slowly around the fortress. They were careful not to make any sounds and stayed out of sight of any lookouts. When they reached the large iron gates of the fortress, they found a narrow road that led deep into the forest. Surely this road would take them to the harbor they wanted to find. They would have to be careful to not be seen in any way, and they would have to watch for supply wagons or patrols that might travel the road. They would travel in the night, using the cover of darkness, and were glad the sun was already setting.

The men traveled all night and into the next day, making slow progress as they fought their way through the brush. They saw two different patrols along the edge of the road, but they were able to remain under cover and were not detected. The guards gave no indication that they were searching for anyone, so Baqash felt confident that their presence on the island had not been discovered. He hoped they could keep it that way.

They reached the end of the road at mid-afternoon and found it had led them to a cover where piers had been built for the loading and unloading of sea barges. Wagons could drive right up to the side of a barge and receive the freight directly. There were two barges standing partially loaded at the pier, apparently waiting for a full load to return to the mainland. It reminded Baqash of Bodand's barge before it left Meditrainia. Were leviathans hampering their operations here as well?

The important thing for the two intruders was that each barge had enough cargo for them to hide in on the decks. Baqash had planned to wait until dark before easing himself and Megado into the water and making their way onto the deck from the opposite side of the pier. They would conceal themselves among the bundles until they got to the mainland. It could not be more than a few miles away from the coast.

Night was fully fallen, and the guards around the pier were standing watch at various points. The two men had made their way around the cove where they could enter the water unseen. They eased themselves to the side of a barge from the water side. From there they hoped to pull themselves onto the barge without being detected.

While making their way around the cove, they did not notice the group of guards that had sneaked quietly into the pier area and was waiting, unseen, for Baqash and Megado to make their move. The makeshift raft had been discovered on the other side of the island, and troops had been sent to watch for a getaway from the pier area. They had hidden themselves on the barges to wait for an escape attempt.

When it seemed the coast was clear and being unaware that they had been discovered, the two fugitives made their move. As they climbed over the side to establish their hiding place, a few guards jumped from behind crates with nets, covering the men before they realized what was happening. Unable to react quickly enough, they were clubbed into a daze of confusion, fear, frustration, and desperation, entangled like fish taken in a catch.

As they lay on the deck, the guards laughed, cursed, and boasted over the success of the shrewd tactics that had awarded them this catch. They removed the nets and tied ropes around the captives' necks. The ropes ran down their backs and tied their hands behind them. The guards slapped and kicked and abused the men until both were bruised and bleeding. The leader began to interrogate them when they looked like they were conscious enough to talk. "Who are you? What are your names? Where do you come from? What are you doing on this forbidden island?" The leader was in their faces and forced them to stand on their knees while men behind them pulled their heads back with their hair. The leader yelled at them over and over again, slapping them when they did not answer.

He then checked them for the mark of the serpent and found they had none. "So you have no serpent's mark. You are criminals of the temple. Where are your marks, you worthless stench? Stand them up, and we will take them to the fortress. We'll get something out of them there."

They jerked the two captives to their feet and walked them off the huge barge and away from the pier. Baqash and Megado made no sound as they began their forced march back to the training fortress of the Violent Ones. By now they were in so much pain and were so delirious from their beatings that they could only concentrate on staying on their feet as they tried to keep up with the wagon they were tied behind. Their captors jeered at them and whipped them as they dragged them along the road. After a while, everything became a blur as they stumbled on, their every move nothing more than a reflex.

Twelve

The Island Fortress

Baqash woke and found himself lying on the hard dirt floor of a cage-like cell. He had no idea how long he had been lying there, but it seemed as though it was the middle of the afternoon, at least a day or two after he and Megado had been abducted. His body ached from the beating he had endured, but his wounds were already healing fairly well. The heavy atmospheric pressure was doing its work. His wounds were turning into scars because they had not been cleaned with water, but the aches and pains were overshadowed by the tremendous hunger he had developed during his long, unconscious recovery.

As he regained awareness of what was happening around him, Baqash realized he was imprisoned in the fortress in a group of cages next to the high wall, not far from a combat training ground. There were instruments of battle training hanging on storage poles that surrounded a clearing. The equipment was oversized, obviously made to fit the already large young Violent Ones. As he looked around he saw Megado sitting on the ground with his head down in another cage several cages away from his.

Baqash stood up and walked around to try to regain some

strength and gather his thoughts. He stretched his arms in the air and then stretched his back and legs. He tried to get Megado's attention as he walked around to let him know he was all right. He hit the side of the cage a few times to make a little noise for Megado to hear.

As Baqash saw Megado look up and then stand to acknowledge his master, a voice behind him spoke softly but harshly. "No need to worry about him. You'd better worry about yourself, fool."

Baqash turned to see the bent shadow of an old man, his bearded face scarred and dirty. He was standing outside Baqash's cage, leaning against it with his nose protruding between the bars. His eyes were glassy and cold, and the few teeth left in his mouth were a dingy yellow. He was covered in filthy rags and had shackles locked around his ankles; it was clear by the large ugly calluses on his skin that he had worn them for a long time. The man was holding some cabbage leaves, which he threw into the cage for Baqash to eat.

Baqash rushed to the side of the cage where the old man stood and asked, "Who are you, old man?"

"There is no need for you to know my name, doomed one. You and your friend over there will not be around long enough for it to matter. I've been a slave of the temple priests for many revolutions around the sun and seen the likes of you come and go. You will be no different. They will kill you here or send you to die in the arena at Hellsrun. You will have no choice."

At that moment a fortress guard ran to the pitiful looking creature and knocked him to the ground, yelling, "How many times have you been told not to talk to the prisoners, you worthless trash of an old man?" He struck the old man with several lashes of his whip and then kicked him. "Get up and go give that other prisoner some leaves. Then get back to your work!"

Baqash stood and watched as the slave got up and hurried over to Megado's cage. The guard turned to Baqash, put his face against the cage bars, and yelled, "You will not talk to anyone unless you are told to! Next time I'll beat you to shreds!" He turned and walked away, taking his guard position not far from Baqash's cage.

The hunger in Baqash's stomach cried out as he picked up the cabbage leaves and brushed them off. He knew he had to eat whatever was given to him. He had to sustain whatever strength he could. Doomed or not, he was not going to allow his captors to do him in without a struggle. He ate the cabbage and was glad to get it.

Several rotations of the earth went by, and the two men were left to themselves, but Baqash and Megado could only communicate with each other with their eyes. Once a rotation the old slave brought cabbage leaves for them to eat. In bits of stolen conversation Baqash learned that the old man had chosen to be a slave for life rather than try to win his freedom in the arena at Hellsrun. He had spent all his captivity on this island as a forced laborer in the fortress. The slave knew that his captors would kill him one day when he could no longer do the work they expected him to do.

The prisoners watched as the young giants learned methods of combat and mastered the weapons of battle. They also attended classes in which the priests taught them the dark secrets of Lucifer and their heritage as sons of fallen angels. They looked like overgrown men, but they were animals with no conscience. They reveled in their total depravity and looked forward to the day when they could go into the world and use the skills they had learned in their diabolical school.

Each fortress handled no more than four giants at a time. One young student in this fortress was already as large as Hercineolas, the Violent One Adoniel had killed at Hellsrun, and he was still growing. He dominated his peers with his strength and cunning. The priest bragged that they were training the next champion of the arena at Hellsrun.

One day the captors fastened shackles on Baqash and Megado and put them to work cleaning the latrines, washing the cookware in the kitchen, and doing all the dirty work there was to be done. They continued to stay in the cages at night, and cabbage leaves were all they were fed, but they were sometimes able to sneak bites of food from the garbage when the guards were not looking. Their shackles made their ankles blood-raw as they worked from dawn to dusk.

A time came when there was great excitement in the fortress, excitement caused by the anticipation of the arrival of the demonic father of the great young Violent One. He was going to materialize as a human and visit his offspring. This was not a common practice because most demonic parents had no interest in their progeny. But because this Violent One was so unusual, word had gotten out about his unique powers, and the demon wanted to gloat over his special descendent.

The day came for the fallen angel to arrive. Baqash and Megado were left in their cages to be kept out of the way, but they would be able to see the demon as he passed the cages on his way to the training ground. There the young giant would show his strength.

Everyone in the fortress made up the crowd that followed the demon parent and his unnatural child into the arena. They had been at the large meeting hall, having a feast with loud celebration, the result of much wine. Baqash was surprised when he saw the materialized demonic man. The fallen angelic demon was not ugly and hideous-looking in his mortal disguise. Instead, in human form he looked very appealing and was no larger than a normal man. In fact, it would be difficult to pick him out of a crowd. There was a look in his eyes, though, that gave him away. His countenance was sinister and evil.

The young giant performed several acts of strength. He bent spear shafts with his bare hands, lifted large amounts of weight over his head, threw spears at a target, shot an arrow shaft halfway through a tree trunk, and used a sword to chop up whatever got in his way. With each new feat, the fortress priests roared in approval as the young giant demonstrated his developing skills.

The demon parent then raised his hands in disapproval and sneered in a loud, unimpressed voice. "This is all well and good, but can he kill anybody? I want to see some real competition. What can he do in a real battle?"

The head priest smiled proudly at the request. This would be his opportunity to turn his prodigy loose for the first time. "Yes, mighty one," said the priest, gloating. "He is more than ready to shed blood in real combat. Bring some slaves over here and loose them. Give each of them a sword."

Five slaves were brought from the crowd to face the giant. One cried out in fearful protest, "But sir, we became slaves to not have to fight in the arena. We should not be made to fight here."

"Shut him up!" yelled the head priest to a guard next to the slave. The guard reached over and hit the man with a club. The slave fell to his knees.

The crowd made a circle around the practice arena and began to yell as the giant entered the ring with his sword to face five men half his size, untrained and grossly underfed. Baqash could not see the battle from his cage because the crowd blocked his view. He could only see the giant effortlessly wielding his sword, thrusting at his victims. He knew when each slave had fallen by the cheers of the crowd and the hideous laugh of the demon in human form. It was not long until the slaughter was over.

The demon parent was still not satisfied. "That was not at all what I had in mind. If he is to be a great warrior, I want to see him do something spectacular. You have other giant warriors here. I want to see him fight two at once—to the death. If he is great, he will overcome. Those he kills are not worth living anyway if they together cannot kill one Violent One."

The head priest agreed. This would give his student a reputation that would go before him to Hellsrun, and his trainer would be elevated as well. "There are three others besides this one, sir. We will cast lots to see who fights him."

"No!" yelled the demon. "I want the two biggest and best."

"As you wish, sir," the head priest replied approvingly.

The two oldest and largest giants prepared to fight the would-be champion. They all welcomed the chance to finally fight for real, for they did not care about each other. They only cared for themselves and took the challenge with great excitement. They were young and foolish, and the crowd made them braver than their ability. This was a great chance to prove themselves.

The three young giants faced off in full battle armor of helmets, breastplates, and chin guards; each carried a shield with one hand and a sword with the other. Spears had been jammed into the ground nearby for easy access as well. The competitors stalked one another, working up the nerve to begin their attack. The one giant was much larger and stronger than the two he faced, but they had a chance if they fought together.

Again Baqash could only see the three giants that stood head and shoulders above the crowd, and they put on a great show for their diabolical guest. There was much destruction done to the area enclosed by the arena, and the crowd roared and cheered as they jumped out of the way when the battle raged close to them. The demon laughed with relish at the bloody spectacle he had caused. He lusted over the blood, the sweat, and the sounds of struggle for life. The groans of pain and the force of the clashing swords and shields made him laugh in sinister glee.

The larger giant proved to be too much for the lesser ones. He finished off one with his sword, leaving his weapon protruding from the smaller giant's bowels. Then he grabbed a spear to battle his remaining opponent. When the massacre was finished, the giant raised his fist in triumph, giving a loud growl of exaltation while the crowd went wild with cheers. The demon-man laughed and danced and glared at the gruesome sight of those fallen in battle at the hand of his offspring. He was obviously very pleased with himself and the destruction he had brought about in the fortress.

The crowd finally moved away from the battle area and returned to feasting. Their laughter and celebration could be heard in the background as Baqash stood and looked at the remains of the slain. He felt sick to his stomach as he looked at the sight, knowing that it would be his and Megado's job to burn the remains. He wondered, *Why didn't they force Megado and me to fight the young killer? There must be a reason. But it is likely one I don't want to know.*

The drunken celebration became another brawl in the background as Baqash sat in his cage. He could hear the fighting, cursing, and boisterous laughter well into the night, but the dead bodies lay where they had fallen, with unimpressed eyes. They no longer celebrated. They only continued to deteriorate in death. Baqash wondered if he would meet his end in a similar way.

It was late in the afternoon of the next rotation that Baqash and Megado were pressed, along with several other slaves, into putting the corpses of the two young giants and the five human slaves onto wagons to be taken outside the fortress for burning. By now the bodies emitted a strong stench of rotting flesh. After being taken to the hole that had been dug by other slaves next to the forest line, the bodies were unceremoniously dumped in it and burned. Baqash and Megado helped cover up the ashes, the grave making a small mound above the ground. The leftover waste of the demon's lust for blood had been disposed of. The slaves who had participated in the burial were taken to the seaside on a forced march and made to wash off in the water so they would not contaminate the fortress.

Baqash and Megado had been held in the fortress for almost a full revolution around the sun. They had been beaten, interrogated about their reasons for being on the forbidden island, and worked to exhaustion. They continued to maintain their story of being shipwrecked by a leviathan, but because they had no mark of the serpent, they were not believed. They were spies, enemies of the serpent.

The time came when a group of guards came to escort Baqash and Megado to see the head priest of the fortress. His headquarters were in a fortified complex next to the temple area to protect him from any possible revolts from slaves or Violent Ones. The inside was covered with plush decorations of fur, serpent idols, gold, and silver. Jewel-laden objects dotted the walls.

The two slaves were made to stand before the head priest as he sat on a throne-like judgment seat before them. They were forced to kneel in his presence. He glared at Baqash and Megado momentarily, his grin suggesting that he relished the control he had over them. He felt great satisfaction because of the news he was about to personally give his captives.

"I know who you are. I have been waiting for word from the temple at Hellsrun concerning you, and it finally came with the last shipment of supplies. It seems I have made myself a great hero in the eyes of the high priest because of you two. He has been looking for you for quite some time now, and I have the power to deliver

you to him. He was very pleased to learn that the son of Cainogan
and his slave had finally been captured. He looks forward to seeing
you both take your stand in the arena against his new champion.
The high priest was very displeased at your involvement in the
escape of one named Dago and your own failure to take the vow of
submission to Lucifer.

"I have orders to send you and this slave to Hellsrun immediately. You are to leave with the next barge returning to the mainland. When you reach shore, you will be taken by a temple guard to
Hellsrun. There you will have no choice but to fight in the arena to
your death." The priest looked over at two guards and ordered, "Take
them back to the cages, and get them ready to leave at the next rising of the sun."

As the two prisoners walked back to their cages, Baqash was at
first stunned by the anguish he felt at the thought of having to go
back to Hellsrun. It was a place he had hoped to never see again.
Now I know why they did not force us to fight the young Violent One,
he thought. *They were waiting to get word from Hellsrun before they
tried to dispose of us.* As he thought further, a ray of hope began to
sparkle in his heart. *This is our chance. We won't have to try to escape
from the island because the temple guards will take us to the mainland.
We could have been killed here, but now they are moving us. There
will be many more chances for escape while traveling to Hellsrun than
there have been here in the fortress. Yes, this is our chance!*

These thoughts reverberated in Baqash's mind as he and Megado moved quickly along the path back to the cage. He felt encouraged within himself and fought hard not to let his newfound excite-

ment show. For the first time in a long time, he thought again about the God of Adoniel. The thought that he might yet get to see the garden caught him by surprise as it slipped into his conscience. He had forgotten how much that search had meant to him. The fire was being rekindled.

Thirteen

The Prison Wagon

At the rising of the sun, when the mist came up from the ground to water the earth, guards came to the cages. They opened the doors and put a steel band around the necks of Baqash and Megado. Chains attached the neck bands to bands that locked on their wrists like huge bracelets. The shackles on their ankles were left in place, and they were ready for their journey.

The two slaves were tied to the back of a wagon that pulled them down the road to the pier where they had first begun their captivity many rotations ago. The wagon moved slowly enough to allow them to trot along without being dragged on the ground, and their guards followed behind in another wagon. The mist made the road cool and soft as they jogged along in their bare feet.

At the pier the prisoners were locked in a cell on the bottom deck of the barge. A guard stood outside by the door while slaves from the fortress loaded the cargo that was going to the mainland. It was the first time Baqash and Megado had been left alone since their abduction.

The two men looked at each other as they sat on the floor of the barge. They had been through a great deal together, yet now they were almost like strangers to one another. They were filthy, their hair long and disheveled, their long beards thick and matted with the accumulated grime of their captivity. They sat quietly for a moment, looking at one another. Then both grinned in unison like two boys who had just pulled something over on their tutor.

"Megado," whispered Baqash, trying to keep the guard from hearing, "do you know what this means?"

Megado was puzzled by his master's excited question. He had no idea what the situation meant except that they were being taken to Hellsrun to die, but Baqash's excitement ignited his curiosity. "No , Master. What does it mean?"

"On this journey we will have a much better chance to escape than we would have had on the island. By being moved, we have been given some time to possibly make a break. This could be our reprieve, Megado."

"No, Master, I had not seen this move in that way. I had resigned myself to the thought that we were doomed to die in Hellsrun. You give me hope that I will still have opportunity to vindicate myself in my own eyes. Maybe I can redeem myself in your eyes as well from my foolish blunder when we first traveled to Hellsrun many revolutions ago."

"Megado, you have been a brave warrior through all we have encountered. You have more than redeemed yourself in my eyes. You are a worthy and valuable slave to me."

"No, Master, what you say comes from a heart that has been to the pit and back. I thank you for your kindness to me in what you say, but I will know within myself when I have put all things in balance again."

The two men stared forward at the door of their cell as they waited for the barge to move. They were filled with a mix of hope and concern about where this new twist in their ordeal would take them. Wherever that was, each man felt for the moment that it was good to have someone other than an enemy sitting next to him.

The time came for the barge to be loosed from the pier. They could hear men calling out to each other as they made preparations to leave port. The barge gave a jump as the paddle wheels began to turn under the force of the team of elephants walking on the treadmill. This was a much larger barge than Bodand's, for the operations of the temple of the serpent around the world could afford the more costly kinds of items available to man.

It only took one full rotation of the earth to make it to the mainland. The island was closer to the mainland than Baqash had first estimated, but it was still far enough away that escape from the island would have been almost impossible. Baqash, though, saw the barge ride as the solution to that big problem.

The barge was tied to the pier of a small town called Deddi on the east coast of the Prime Meridian Sea. The guards took their captives to a prison compound and checked them in. Baqash and Megado were put in separate cells to wait until they could be turned over to a guard detail that would hook up with a caravan going to Hellsrun. Prisoners were often moved in prison wagons by temple guards under the protection of a caravan rather than traveling independently. They did not need as many guards that way, and the risk of being attacked by road thugs was reduced.

Baqash and Megado stayed in the jail compound for several rotations. The food was a little better, and they had a chance to rest and regain some strength. Finally Baqash saw an iron wagon with barred door and windows pulled up in front of the jail. The time had come to start the long trip to Hellsrun at the northernmost point of the earth. Deddi was just north of the equator, so the journey would cover half the hemisphere—if they should go all the way to Hellsrun, that is.

The inside of the wagon was an empty, iron-walled shell with a hard wooden floor. It was not built for comfort. The best a passenger could do when riding was sit on the floor, lean against a wall, and try not to get knocked around against the walls opposite each other. Baqash and Megado looked around the inside of the wagon as the door of bars slammed shut. They were beginning to adjust to the steel collars they were wearing although their necks were still a little raw. Inside the wagon the two men could talk freely and not be heard above the road noise caused by the wagon. Baqash continued to study the wagon to see if there were any weaknesses that could be exploited. At first glance he could see none. "We need to be on the alert, looking for every possible moment that could be our chance of escape. There has to be a way out of here," he said, carefully inspecting the wagon.

"How can we hope to fight or run when we are tied by these chains?" asked Megado with a hint of frustration.

"We will travel through many constellations of the stars before we reach Hellsrun, and we will have many rotations to discover weaknesses in our guards' care of us. When the time comes, we will take advantage of those weaknesses."

Baqash sat for a long time looking at his chains and the shackles on his ankles. As he studied them, he made an observation: the steel bands around his wrists and ankles had a small corner on the outside edge that was fairly sharp, and this gave him an idea. "Megado, I think I know what we can do about these chains. Do you see that sharp edge on your wrist and ankle bands? I can take a link of chain on your shackles and rub it on your wrist band. It will take a long time, but I think it will eventually cut through. I can saw your chains and you can saw mine, but we will not sever them all the way through until we are ready with a plan of escape. For now we will cut the links close to the bands so that when we are ready, we can break the chains and be free to fight and run. We can even use the chains as weapons if we need to. Come over here, and let me try to score a beginning notch."

Megado moved slowly to Baqash, who sat in a corner of the wagon so as not to be seen by the guards riding outside. Baqash began to rub the chain link on the edge of the steel band. After several short, clumsy strokes, a mark appeared on the chain link. The two men looked at it and then at each other, grinning. It would take a long time, but time was something they had plenty of.

"What we will need to do is work in short intervals and then get up and walk around so the guards can see us and not become suspicious of our activity. Hopefully they will not feel a need to check our chains."

After saying this, Baqash went to work on Megado's chain. Megado picked up Baqash's chain and began as well. They rubbed feverishly for a short period of time and then stood up and walked around in the wagon so the guards would be sure to see them. They continued this process for several rotations, taking breaks whenever the wagon stopped and they were taken out to walk around. They also took breaks to eat whatever small portions of food they were given. They made slow progress at cutting through their chains, but the more they worked at it, the more proficient they became at the task.

During this time the wagon had been traveling up the coast of the Prime Meridian Sea, working its way toward Krin where they could join a caravan going north to Hellsrun. They had overheard the guards talking about their travel plans when they had made a previous stop. Baqash had hoped to make it to Krin but not in a prison wagon. Then again, Bodand never did make it to Krin. At least in the prison wagon Baqash could still fight to stay alive.

Krin was a large seaport city much like Meditrainia. It lay on the northeast coast of the Prime Meridian Sea, and the Tropic of Cancer Highway passed through it. This made the city a prime stop for caravans in their worldwide travels. The prison wagon would easily find a caravan to travel with the rest of the way.

There was going to be a wait in Krin for several rotations because the next caravan going to Hellsrun would not be ready to leave until then. During that time, the prisoners would remain locked in the wagon, taken out once a day to relieve themselves. They had to work more quietly on their chains since the wagon was no longer moving and the guards were standing just outside the door. They were much encouraged, though, because they were making progress.

Fourteen

The Escape

On the third rotation, when the sun was in the middle of the sky, another prison wagon pulled alongside the wagon Baqash and Megado were being held in. Their head guard seemed surprised as he asked, "What is this all about?"

"We got one of those religious weirdos going to Hellsrun. He claims to be some kind of Sethite. He don't believe in Lucifer. He refused to make the journey to Hellsrun to receive the mark of the serpent," said the driver matter-of-factly.

"Well, he ought to enjoy his ride with these two we got in here. They refused the mark and helped another prisoner escape from the arena. You know, I can't imagine what goes through these kooks' minds to make them do the stupid things they do," the guard replied, shaking his head.

"Well, whatever it is, I sure can't see how it could be worth ending up in the arena at Hellsrun," answered the driver as he climbed down from the prison wagon.

The prisoner from the newly arrived wagon was in chains like those Baqash and Megado wore. The guards brought the man around to their wagon, opened the door, and shoved him in. The man crawled over to the side of the wagon and sat on the floor. "Well," he said, "it sounds like we have more things in common than these chains."

Baqash and Megado had dropped their work when the other prison wagon pulled up and were looking out the small barred windows on the side of the wagon during the prisoner transfer. They sat down tentatively and leaned against the wall opposite their new prison mate. Baqash did not respond to the man immediately, instead choosing to size him up first. He had learned to be cautious from all that he and Megado had endured, and it would be awhile before he knew if this man could be trusted with their secret plans to escape. His presence certainly made Baqash's plan more complicated, at least for the time being.

The man's face was gaunt, and he was thinly built and small in stature. He looked as if he had been in captivity for a long time. His hair was long and stringy, as was his beard, and those of his teeth that had not been knocked out during a beating were discolored. There was a large, ugly scar over his left eye that had healed without being tended to. It was clear this man was not a warrior, for in the few words he had spoken, he sounded more like a man of intellect than a man of battle.

"I don't blame you for being suspicious of me," said the stranger in reply to their silence. "In this world it is hard to know whom a person can trust. We have to be careful to whom we give ourselves." He paused a moment to see if Baqash and Megado would reply and then continued. "My name is Shadi. I am of the line of Seth, son of Adam. My father is Irad, son of Enoch. Enoch sits on the council of the Line of Light. We worship the one true Creator, Elohim. That is why I am in these chains. I have never made the journey to Hellsrun to fulfill the Holy Rite of Passage to receive my mark. I was a tender of sheep in my father's household. We try to stay to ourselves and not venture far from our family. In that way we protect ourselves from encountering the priests of the serpent. They hunt continually, so we have to stay on the move as much as we can. I was caught in a raid by temple warriors while out in the pasture with my sheep two revolutions ago. I have been a slave on a temple farm close to Narvin on the lower Gihon River since that time. The high priest in Hellsrun has decided to make a spectacle of all those connected with the Line of Light. Those captured will automatically be sent to the arena for judgment. From what the guard said, I understand you are fugitives of the temple as well."

Baqash had heard these names before. He was intrigued by the possibility of meeting another Sethite. Maybe this man knew of Adoniel. What a wonder it would be if that were true! Baqash spoke slowly and with reservation. "Would you have known a man named Adoniel? He was the son of Methuselah, son of Enoch in the line of Seth. He spoke to me of the Line of Light."

"You know of Adoniel? His father and my father are brothers! We grew up together. He is a mighty man of faith, and he was going to Hellsrun to preach and teach of Elohim. It was his dream to spread the truth of Elohim there. His friend Dago had committed to go with him as protector. I was captured before they left the Four Forks in the River, and I have heard nothing of them since then."

Baqash truly was astounded as he looked at the cousin of Adoniel the Sethite. Here was a man who could take him to the Four Forks in the River. He could introduce him to the Line of Light. Maybe this man had seen the garden. "Adoniel and Dago are the reason we are in these chains today," said Baqash. He then told the story of how he had met Adoniel and how he and Megado had seen his victorious death. He told of helping Dago escape and of his decision to reject taking the vow of the serpent. Baqash then explained how he had been rejected at Cainogan and had set out on his journey to find the Garden of Eden that Adoniel had told him about.

Shadi's eyes began to water as Baqash told his story. By the time he finished, the Sethite was in tears. All the emotions of being separated from his family for so long with no hope of escape, hearing the news of Adoniel, and seeing these two men sitting with him as fruits of the life and death of a close relative had overwhelmed him. He wept for some time as Baqash and Megado allowed him his time of release.

As he watched this man in tears, Baqash thought about the situation. He could not believe he had completely opened up to this man so quickly. He could not believe that he felt compassion for him and his tears instead of disgust at what he would have seen as a weakness not long ago.

After gathering himself together, Shadi spoke. "Elohim has truly been my guide. How wonderful are His ways! He truly directs the path of the righteous and overthrows the schemes of those who are evil in His sight. His hand has been on me to bring me to this place. I have the great task of finishing the work begun by my dearly beloved Adoniel."

Baqash spoke again. "Whether or not this Elohim has brought you here, I do not know. I know we are here in a prison wagon and must have a plan to break free soon. The longer we wait, the harder it will be to escape. It may be that we should plan our escape before we are connected to a caravan and have many more guards with whom we must contend." Baqash could not believe what he had just said. He thought, *This man has only been in my presence a short time, and I've already revealed our plan to escape. He may not be strong enough to carry out the plan. What if he gets nervous and makes a slip that alerts the guards to our plan? It's too late now. I have to move on. We may have to kill this man if he becomes a hindrance. What task was he talking about anyway?*

"We make our plans," continued Shadi, "but Elohim brings them to pass. If your plan comes from Him, then you will succeed. What is your plan? Maybe I can help you in it."

Baqash had a decision to make. Should he reveal the whole plan to this man? Something told him that he could move forward and trust this Sethite. "I am going to put our lives in your hands, Shadi, and let you know my plan. If you fail me in this trust, I will have to kill you. Do you understand?"

"I am already a dead man in this prison wagon. My life has been put in your hands by Elohim, and I know that you are my salvation. My deliverance has been given to you just as Dago has found life by your hand. If we can escape, I can finish the task given me by Elohim."

"What is this task you speak of?" asked Baqash, annoyed by the mysterious words of this man, Shadi.

"You know my task better than I. I am to take you to my family and help you come to the truth that has been planted in your heart by my beloved Adoniel. Then he will not have died in vain."

Baqash looked at the man, puzzled. How did Shadi know that he had had those thoughts? He remembered how Adoniel had shown a similar kind of discernment.

Before Baqash could respond to Shadi, Megado uncharacteristically spoke up without being acknowledged. "I have come to believe in your Elohim. He is my God."

What is happening here? thought Baqash, jerking his head to look at Megado, whom he had almost forgotten was in the wagon. He felt threatened by his slave's boldness. He gritted his teeth and said, "You will speak when spoken to. Remember who you are, slave." Megado bowed his head and did not reply.

Shadi looked at Megado and then back at Baqash. He gave a slight smile and asked, "What is your plan, my friend?"

Baqash showed Shadi the chains on his ankles and wrists where Megado had rubbed them halfway through. Then he reached over and showed him Megado's chains as well. When Shadi saw the chains were nearly cut through, his eyes grew large with astonishment. It was as if he could not believe what he was seeing.

"We have been working on these chains for three rotations. We must cut through them more so when we are ready, we can break them with a jerk and surprise attack the guards when they take us out of the wagon. We should be ready in one more rotation. Now that you are here, I think this is what we will do. We will continue to work on the chains until the next time the guards open the door on the morrow. Then we will break the chains and overpower them as we climb out. There will be no more than three. We will shove them into the wagon, tie them, gag them, and take their clothing for ourselves. Megado and I will put on their clothes and harness the team of rhinoceroses. Shadi, you will stay in the wagon with the guards because we will not have time to cut your chains now. We will drive the wagon away as if we were the guards moving to another position, but we will have to move quickly and not make much noise."

"That is an Elohim-inspired plan," said Shadi. "I am sure it will work." He nodded his head in approval. Megado nodded in agreement as well. He moved next to Baqash and began to work on his chains; Baqash joined him in the task. Shadi looked out the wagon window to make sure the guards were not suspicious.

The men worked feverishly through the night and into the next day, taking short breaks and moving around occasionally so the guards would not become curious. The links in the chains they were cutting were almost to the point that a quick jerk would snap them when the time for evening relief drew near. "All right," said Baqash, "do you understand what we are about to do? There will be no turning back once we make our move." He looked intently into his fellow prisoners' eyes as they nodded their heads.

"I shall say a prayer," said Shadi as they huddled together. Prayer was the last thing on Baqash's mind, but he did not resist the suggestion. Maybe a prayer would help if this God Elohim had the power to help or cared to help.

"O mighty Elohim," said Shadi, "the Creator and Protector of those who love you with a whole heart, You see our bonds, and You know our hearts. We are here because we have chosen to follow You. Give us Your strength and protection as we seek to overcome our enemies. You are our strong arm and deliverer. We give You praise. So be it." They did not have time to say another word, for the guards were just outside the door.

One of the guards unlatched the door of bars. They were talking and laughing with each other, not suspecting a thing. They had gone through this routine enough that they now took it for granted. Baqash stepped out first and positioned himself away from the wagon with the three guards between it and him. Next Megado stepped out, being careful not to break his chains too soon. Shadi hesitated inside, acting like he was afraid to leave the wagon. One of the guards stuck his head in the door to yell at Shadi more directly and put a foot up to climb inside. As he started into the wagon, Shadi grabbed him and pulled him through the door. He held the guard close to his body as they struggled on the wagon floor, trying to keep the man from giving him a direct blow.

For a split second, the other two guards turned their heads, watching their partner as he began to climb into the wagon. When they did, Baqash and Megado jerked the chains on their wrists and necks loose, reached down, and grabbed the chains between their ankles. As they came up from their bent-over position, the two guards turned back to see them straightening up. The prisoners pulled the chains from their ankles and across the faces of the guards, knocking them into the side of the wagon. They hit them under the chin with their fists to give them knockout blows, and then they hit them again to be sure they were unconscious. Baqash jumped into the wagon where Shadi was about to take a beating from the guard who was breaking free from his grasp. Baqash hit the guard on the side of the head with his fists clasped together. The guard recovered and turned to face him, but Baqash hit him again with a solid blow, knocking him out like the others.

Baqash then jumped out of the wagon and helped Megado shove the two guards inside. They removed the clothes from two of their captives and then bound all three, tying their hands and feet together with the newly broken chains. Then they stuffed wads of cloth in the men's mouths so they could not call out when they awakened.

Baqash and Megado put on the guards' clothes. How different it felt to have on something half clean! They slowly looked out the wagon door to see if their scuffle had drawn any attention. Dusk was approaching, and in the parked wagon area, people were getting ready to eat or go into the city. All was well.

Baqash motioned to Megado, and they walked behind the wagon where the rhino team was penned. They found the lead rhino and harnessed it and then lined up each of the other five in position and harnessed them as well. Then they led the team to the front of the wagon and hitched them to the wagon's tongue. The animals were large beasts and stood taller than Baqash, who was positioned between a pair of them to make connections while Megado was on the outside, pulling the reins from the bits in the animals' mouths up to the driver's seat. Baqash did not see the arrival of the other two guards who were patrolling the area.

These guards carried spears and wore swords, and as they drew closer, they stopped to see what was going on at the prison wagon. Hesitating, they began to move toward the wagon more quickly since it seemed strange that guards were harnessing a team to a prison wagon that was not scheduled to leave yet. By this time Megado was in the driver's seat overlooking the team, and he saw the guards approaching. He stayed in the seat as they neared the wagon and alerted Baqash. "Master, there are patrol guards coming."

Baqash had just finished the hook-up, so he jumped onto the tongue and yelled, "Take off!" Megado gave a cry and whipped the team into a fast start while Baqash held his own between the rhinos as they broke into a run. The wagon did not have time to turn, so they were forced to drive close to the guards. As the wagon passed, one of the guards threw his spear at Megado. Baqash looked up at Megado in time to see the spear plunge into his slave's side. Megado leaned over under the force of the spear, but he did not let go of the reins. Instead, he took his left hand and pulled the spear out, trying to prop himself up as he continued to hold the team in line toward an exit from the parking area.

Baqash was frantic. He could not believe his eyes. This was not supposed to happen! Where was this Elohim whom Shadi had prayed to? He cried out, "Megado! Megado!" as he fought to climb into the driver's seat on the fast-moving wagon. He could tell Megado was failing fast, and he had to get up there with him as quickly as he could. "Where is Elohim?" he cried. "Megado believed in You! Megado! Megado!"

Baqash finally got into the seat and took the reins from his slave, who leaned over against the side of the seat as if to say he knew he had finished his task. All Baqash could do was keep driving. He headed straight out of the city, not caring which way he went. He knew the guards would have a troop after them soon, so he did not have much time. As they got left the city on a main road, they entered a forest where there were a lot of trees and no oncoming traffic

Baqash stopped the wagon and called out to Shadi, "Get out of the wagon! Hurry and get out!" He grabbed Megado and slowly pulled him from the driver's seat. By this time blood was everywhere, and Baqash was covered in it as he gently lowered his slave from the wagon and carried him into the thicket at the side of the road. By the time Baqash returned to the wagon, Shadi had hopped out and was standing in the road.

"Go over and take care of Megado, there in the thicket!" demanded Baqash as he ran to the side of the rhino team. "Yah! Yah! Yah!" he yelled, and the team took off. He ran alongside the animals to be sure they kept going. Baqash knew the troops behind would follow the wagon for awhile, and that would give him and his companions time to move deep into the forest. As the prison wagon rambled on down the road, Baqash hurried back to where he had laid Megado.

When he reached his friend, Shadi was bending over Megado and holding his side. Baqash knelt and leaned over the young man and noticed his breathing had become weaker. His body shook periodically, and Megado opened his eyes and looked up at his master. Baqash could tell he was trying to say something, so he leaned over to hear him. Megado's voice was very weak, and he spoke in a whisper as he choked on the blood oozing from his mouth. "I am vindicated. All is well. I am free in Elohim." The dying free man stared into the dusk, gave a slight smile, and relaxed into death.

In that moment Baqash's heart ripped apart. "No, no, no! Not this!" he sobbed. "Not Megado! He is too young! He deserves to live!" He stopped for a moment and looked up at Shadi, meeting his eyes. "I curse the day I met the man called Adoniel! Since I met him, I have lost all that is dear to me! Where was this Elohim when Adoniel needed him most? Who is this God who allows those who love Him the most to suffer the most?" Baqash looked at Shadi in disgust, got up, and walked away. He found a place to sit alone in the falling darkness.

Baqash had no tears. His anger raged in his deepest parts. He wanted to be free of all this. Why couldn't' he have been the one to die? Death in this ugly world was the only true liberation. He knew in the back of his mind that he did not have time for this grief and self-pity, but he just didn't care anymore. He was locked in a prison, for he could no longer go home, he hated the serpent god, Lucifer, and he no longer knew if he wanted to have anything to do with this Elohim. Now he had to deal with the Sethite, Shadi, who was still in chains. His first inclination was to run and leave him there, but somehow something inside him would not let him.

He rose and walked back to where Shadi still knelt over Megado's body. He could hear Shadi praying softly and weeping, but he wanted nothing to do with his tears. "Get up, and let's move the body," said Baqash coldly. He picked up Megado one last time and carried him deeper into the woods, away from the road. As best they could, he and Shadi quickly covered Megado with rocks, branches, and leaves to try to camouflage it from those who might try to track them down.

The two fugitives left the mound they had made and ran into the forest, dodging bushes and ducking under branches with Shadi doing his best to keep up though his ankles were still chained. In the distance they heard a group of mounted troops riding by in pursuit of the stolen prison wagon. Dark had settled and would be the fugitives' friend for the night.

Fifteen

A New Friend

The night in the forest was not as gloomy as the darkness Baqash felt in his heart as his grief truly set in. Only now had he begun to realize how much Megado had come to mean to him. As he looked back on their time together and all they had been through, Baqash realized that he had grown closer to this young slave than to any brother he had ever had. No brother would have sacrificed himself as Megado had done to help him follow his heart.

The two men stopped to rest in the forest. They sat on the cool ground, surrounded by a clump of bushes. Though the light of the moon and stars was enhanced by the vapor canopy, that light was almost completely obscured by the tall trees, with branches grown so thick that even the light of the sun could barely penetrate the darkness.

Baqash sat, thinking of how much he envied Megado. Life had been so simple to him, so uncomplicated by all the problems of ruling and owning and keeping what he had. It seemed so easy for Megado to die with no regrets or unfulfilled expectations. He regained his self-respect, and for him that was enough. This belief Megado had come to have in the God of the Sethites had been so easy for him to embrace, and in its simplicity it had given him peace to die without fear. How easy it had been for Megado to begin to believe in something Baqash had come to question even more through all the trials and tribulations! *How could it have been so easy for him and not for me? What was the difference for him that I have not obtained? Maybe it's because I've learned to make life hard when it's supposed to be simple. Megado was living what I have to learn. Oh, that it could be that simple!*

"I apologize for my anger," Baqash said to Shadi. "I am sure that Megado found strength in your Elohim, strength I have not yet found. I have no guarantee I will ever find what I am looking for. I do not even know exactly what it is I am looking for. I only know I am not satisfied with what I have found in this life up to now."

"Maybe it would be easier to allow it to find you. If there is a God great enough to make you and all you have seen in the creation, don't you think that He is big enough to find you if you want Him to? Could it be that you have already been found and do not even know it?"

The words came softly, the voice of a man Baqash could not see in the darkness. The truth in the words made it seem that more than a man had spoken. He knew that Shadi was there, but maybe, just maybe, more than a man wanted him to hear.

In an instant, the warrior's desire to live was once again awakened. Shoving the moment aside, Baqash said abruptly, "We must keep moving. We need to find a river or stream in which to change our direction. We will make them think that we are heading east in the direction of the Four Forks in the River. We will make tracks in that direction and then go the opposite way in the middle of the stream. After we have gone far enough, we will make a fire and try to cut your chains."

Shadi said nothing when the two men made their way once again through the thick forest undergrowth. After several degrees of time, they came to a stream; above which the early morning sun was trying to break through the gap in the skyline of trees. The two fugitives walked into the middle of the stream and sat down to drink and bathe themselves and their clothes all at the same time. They took a while, allowing the clear, flowing water to invigorate their whole beings. As the dirt and grime of the world washed away from their bodies, they felt a cleansing of their inner beings as well. They were being renewed, and each new minute of freedom gave hope that their escape had been secured.

This was no time, however, to take their freedom for granted. They both made several tracks where they entered the water and ran down the bank of the stream for over a mile. Then they crossed the river and made tracks that again moved east in the thick brush. They climbed up into the trees and moved back north in the opposite direction for several yards until it would be impossible for any pursuers to catch their trail again. It was a lot of hard work for Shadi in his chains, but they finally reentered the stream by crawling on a branch over the water and dropping themselves into it. Next they would travel northwest upstream as far as they could to keep their tracks hidden.

It was extremely difficult for Shadi to travel in the water in his chains. He could walk with almost normal strides, but when he tried to go faster, he had to hop as much as run. They had to find some way to remove his chains before much longer because the shackles were rubbing blisters in the skin close to his already large calluses. Baqash was gaining more and more respect for Shadi as he watched him go through this trial with strength and courage. He was more of a man than his less-than-impressive stature showed, and he had an inner strength that became more and more evident as he strove to keep pace with the born warrior, Baqash.

When they were upstream about a mile above the place where they first came to the stream, they stepped out of the water and walked along the tree line of the dense forest. At night they moved away from the stream several yards into the trees and brush to find food and to sleep. There was an abundance of edible leaves, fruits, and berries to sustain them.

In the thick forest they saw the smaller kinds of wildlife that could move with ease in the thick vegetation. They saw deer, rabbits, squirrels, foxes, some large bears, raccoons, badgers, and otters. There were no animals that posed a threat to them unless the animals felt threatened. There were no carnivores in those days, so the forest was a safe place.

Late one evening as the dark was setting in, Shadi tripped over a huge log that was lying on the forest floor. There was something strange about this log that lay almost as high as a man's knee across the ground with both ends extending into the bushes. When Shadi rolled over and looked back to see what he had stumbled over, he saw that the log had a beautiful design on its back, and it began to move slowly away. It crawled and crawled and crawled until about

fifty feet of log had passed in front of Shadi, who sat quietly watching. It was an anaconda, apparently browsing along the forest floor
for fallen fruit and nuts to eat. Shadi stood up and looked in the direction that the snake was moving. He saw a large head rise twenty
feet in the air from the bushes twenty feet in the air and look back,
its a long forked tongue jutting from its mouth. It paused for a moment and hissed loudly, its mouth open wide, and then lay down to
continue on its way. As his composure returned, Shadi thought, *It
is a good thing that the animals Elohim made are not mean like men.
There are many beasts in this world that could do man much harm.*

The next day as the two escapees followed the stream, they
noticed that the land was beginning to slope upward, and the
found themselves climbing a hill. The water in the stream moved
more rapidly down the hill, over and around the rocks in its path.
They topped the forest-covered hill, only to find they had come to
the place of the stream's origin: a beautiful, crystal-clear lake fed
by springs flowing from underground. The lake looked like a large,
round laver that had water spilling over its sides, creating streams in
all directions, just like the one they had been following.

Wildlife abounded everywhere they looked. A herd of duckbill
dinosaurs scooped plankton from the shallow bottoms near the
shore, large alligators and crocodiles lay in the soothing pink light,
and long-necked diplodocuses and brachiosaurs waded in the deep
water, their long necks looking like snakes walking on water. All
kinds of birds flew overhead, making their unique calls, including
three web-winged pterodactyls in a group. They all had wingspans
of over thirty feet, and their loud, shrieking calls were almost deaf-

ening. The two men stood for several minutes and gazed at the overwhelming exhibit of creation's majesty and variety.

They could hardly believe their eyes. Shadi shifted his weight slightly, causing his chains to rattle and break their concentration. At that moment, Baqash looked at those bands and chains and was struck with the realization that the shackles had become the symbol of the great contradiction of their lives. They were in a world so full of beauty, freedom, and peace, yet they themselves stood in chains. In a moment Baqash's heart knew that man had put the chains on them, not the Creator.

They scanned the shore of the lake, barely able to see the other side. They felt a sense of peace that there was no sign of man anywhere, and Baqash looked at Shadi and said softly, "I would like to spend some time in this place. We will find somewhere to camp away from the stream. If someone has followed us, he will come to the lake as we have, and he may not try to hunt us down. He may decide to wait until we appear again in a city somewhere and try to catch us then. Whatever happens, we need to find a way to rid ourselves of these bands and chains."

The men moved to the other side of the lake before it became dark. Making a clearing in the forest several yards from the shore of the lake, they gathered some food and sat down to a meal from the forest. They went to sleep and slept soundly for the first time since their escape.

The next rotation Baqash made a fire and then found some sharp-edged rocks he could use as tools to cut Shadi's chains. He then took a large gourd and made a pot that would hold water.

After wrapping Shadi's ankle in a wet cloth, he heated the chain links in the fire, re-wetting the cloth periodically. He blew on the fire like a bellows to heat the iron, placed the hot metal on a flat rock, and hit it with the sharp edge of another rock. Finally he was able to break the chains, but the bands around their necks, wrists, and ankles remained. Still, what a relief it was for Shadi to at least have the restriction of the chains removed! As the final link was broken, he gave a deep sigh and said, "Praise the Lord Elohim!"

The men had been so caught up in breaking the chains that they did not notice what was happening around them. The moment Shadi breathed his final word of praise, a band of ten men jumped from the brush around them, shoving spears in their faces and around their heads.

Baqash looked up, stunned but was relieved to see that the men surrounding them were not temple guards. They were a rough-looking lot to be sure, but before he could get a better glimpse, a blindfold was jerked around his eyes. His hands were tied behind his back, and he was grasped under the arms, lifted to his feet, and led away. Stumbling along with Shadi behind him, Baqash thought, *Man lurks even in paradise.*

The group walked for at least an hour, the branches slapping them as they moved through the thick undergrowth. The men who led them did not speak. Though they pushed and shoved their captives to keep them moving, they were not mean and cruel like the guards who had taken Baqash and Megado to the fortress on the island after they had been captured at the pier. Baqash wondered over and over who these men were, but there was no way of really knowing until they got to where they were being led. One thing was certain: whatever their destination, these men wanted to be sure Baqash and Shadi had no idea where it was.

After a while, the terrain began to change, and the group began climbing a narrow trail with a rock wall along one side. They stopped for a few minutes, and it sounded like the men were moving branches and opening a large door. They were then taken into what seemed like a corridor that echoed like a cave. Baqash could tell it was narrow because his shoulders rubbed on either side if he bent to one side or the other. He also had to bow his head and bend his knees to keep from grazing his head on the ceiling. This must be some kind of secret passage that led to wherever they were being taken.

As they walked on what seemed to be a downward path, the air got cooler and cooler, and they heard echoing sounds of a large group of people. It was not long until they could walk upright in what felt like a large cavern rather than a tunnel. The guards who escorted the captives began to speak to people who came up to them and asked questions about where they had found these strangers. The leader replied to them, "Be quiet! Don't ask questions. You will know after we make our report to Guydo. Get out of the way!"

They finally came to a stop, and the two captives could hear the crowd growing louder and more restless as they gathered around. "They didn't bring the temple priest with them, did they?"

"Are they spies?"

"Where did you find them?"

"We ought to cut their throats so they won't expose our hiding place." On and on the crowd grumbled as the guards made Baqash and Shadi kneel and then removed their blindfolds.

The cave was dimly lit by torches and wine-generated electric lanterns. The cavern was a huge open space, with high ceilings and large enough to accommodate a few hundred people. It seemed as if at least that many had crowded around to see what was going on.

As Baqash and Shadi knelt, their hands still tied behind their backs, the crowd parted to allow a group of men to make their way to the prisoners. A giant of a man who stood a head taller than all the others stepped forward and came to stand in front of the two men. *This must be the Guydo they spoke of,* thought Baqash as he looked up at this hulking man.

"Where did you capture them?" the man asked in a rich, deep voice, looking down at Baqash and Shadi.

"They were down by the lake in a clearing they had made," replied the leader of the patrol. We were on patrol when we saw the smoke of their fire and heard them breaking the chains from their iron bands."

Guydo stared at the men for a moment, checking every detail of their appearance and demeanor. Then he said, "I do not believe they can be spies planted by the temple priest. Their necks and arms and legs are too heavily callused to have had irons put on recently. They don't have the look of men from the temple either." He looked at Baqash and continued, "You look like the leader. Tell me what you men are doing here."

"Do we have to kneel here like imps before Lucifer's altar? Must we remain with our hands tied as though we were men to be feared by such a great host of people? Are we to be held like fugitives by those who are fugitives themselves?" Baqash replied with the boldness he felt would win the respect of this fellow warrior and obvious enemy of the temple of the serpent. It had become clear to Baqash that this was a hideout of fugitives and criminals running from the law and temple priests.

Guydo laughed and said, "Well, this is the first time I have had a prisoner chide me for treating him like a prisoner." The people around him laughed as well. It looked as if they did just what Guydo wanted them to do. He motioned to his men to untie them, and they stood to their feet.

Baqash then told the story of his rejection of the mark of the serpent, how he had been imprisoned, how he was being sent back to Hellsrun when he met Shadi, and how they had escaped from Krin in the prison wagon. He then told of the death of Megado and how they had fled into the deep forest to escape the temple guards pursuing them.

When he finished telling the story, Guydo put his big hand on Baqash's shoulder and said, "Friend, your story has been told many times over in the lives of us all." He then said to the men who brought them to the cave, "Take these men and cut off their bands. Give them something to eat, and show them a place where they can rest. I will meet with them again on the next rotation."

Later that evening Baqash and Shadi lay on fur pelts they had been given. They still periodically rubbed the places where the bands of iron had been removed. After such a long time of being shackled, it would take awhile to become accustomed to their not being there anymore. They had eaten well and had enjoyed a little good wine. Baqash thought again of Megado and wished that his slave could have enjoyed this freedom before his death.

Shadi spoke and said, "It is Elohim who has taken us by the hand and led us to this place. Bless the Lord God Elohim, Maker of heaven and earth!"

Baqash looked at his new friend in freedom and said, "I am willing to agree that this truly is a great deliverance, but I will not praise Elohim until I see the garden called Eden."

As he lay down to sleep, Baqash's thoughts returned to Cainogan. He thought of growing up in his father's house and the plans he had made to one day rule the province in his father's place with Landua as his wife. Anger began to burn in his heart as he thought of how the tyranny of the serpent god, Lucifer, had totally destroyed all his dreams. He remembered how this bloodthirsty religion had taken his beautiful sister from him and turned his father and promised bride totally against him.

I must find this Garden of Eden in the land where the four rivers fork. I so desire to believe in this God Elohim for whom Adoniel died and who gave so much peace to Megado in dying and to whom Shadi holds so strongly. There must be a God who made the beauty I saw at the lake and in the forest. There must be a God who makes the love I felt for Landua possible. There must be a God who makes me doubt that this bloody Lucifer could ever make any of these things exist. These thoughts filled Baqash's mind as he considered leaving the band of fugitives in the cave. He felt it was time for them to make their move and head to the Land of the Four Forks. He also felt it would be wise to leave as soon as they could, for there was no guarantee that the rebels could remain undetected for a long period of time. He would have to convince Guydo that it would be best for Shadi and him to leave the cave dwellers.

Sixteen

Set the Captives Free

The next day Baqash and Shadi met with Guydo in his dwelling in the cave. They sat on fur pelts in a large room that had walls of cloth. The dwellings in the cave were like tents with no roof over them, and they had separate rooms that used curtains as walls. Many treasures were displayed in various parts of this room; surely it was booty Guydo and his men had taken in raids on caravans and other highway travelers. Seeing these stolen goods everywhere reminded Baqash of the near-fatal attack he and Megado had survived on their trip to Hellsrun. The men who had attacked them were a similar band of thieves and enemies of the serpent temple.

Guydo was very open and friendly to his guests. He talked much of his experience as the chief of his tribe of fugitives. He told of how he had come to be a criminal and organized his gang of social dropouts. The head temple priest at Krin had begun to suspect that Guydo was becoming a threat to his authority because Guydo had questioned some of the priests' practices in over-collecting payments to the temple from the people in Krin. The head priest had tried to have Guydo killed, but he had escaped. The head priest had then taken all his land and livestock as property of the temple. Since that time, Guydo had been helping prisoners escape from the caravans that were taking them to Hellsrun. He also kept in touch with his contacts in Krin to help those escape who had become enemies of the head priest. Guydo had much concern that his hiding place might soon be discovered.

As he listened to the story, Baqash grew confident that Guydo would allow him and Shadi to leave. It was clear that this man was not just a cutthroat thief. He gave the impression that he would understand their desire to finish their trip to Eden.

When Guydo finished his story, Baqash responded. "Guydo, I can see you are a man who has suffered much of what my companion and I have. I think you will understand when I say that Shadi and I are deeply indebted to you and your men for the help you have given us by setting us free from our iron bands of slavery. Shadi and I wore those bands because we would not receive the mark of the serpent. I became a fugitive because I want to believe there is a God higher than the serpent god, Lucifer. I was on a journey to find a garden called Eden in a place called the Four Forks of the River. It is there, I am told, that life began for all men. In the garden is a tree called the Tree of Life, and I must see this garden and the tree before I can truly believe. Shadi is from that land I seek, and we want to continue our journey there."

Guydo shook his head as he pondered what Baqash was asking. "No," he said, "I cannot let you leave this place. I would have to kill you. If you are caught again, the temple priests have ways of getting information from even the strongest and most stubborn men. No, I cannot let you go. I cannot risk our cave's being discovered and our lives being put in jeopardy."

Baqash had an idea. "I can understand your concern, and I would feel the same if I were responsible for all these people. My father is a great lord over his own province, and I have felt the weight of leadership for my people, just as you feel. But, Guydo, when you brought us to this place, we were blindfolded the whole time. Shadi and I have no idea how we got to this place from the lake. What if you put blindfolds on us, have some of your men lead us to a place we do not know, and then leave us to find our way to Eden? If we are caught, we would not be able to tell where this place is even if we wanted to. Your secret would still be safe, and we could continue our journey. With new clothes and boots that cover our scars on our necks, wrists, and ankles, we can travel undetected and have no way of knowing how to return."

"I must think about this," said Guydo, "but until I decide, I will have to keep you under watch. If you try to escape, I will have to kill you." Pausing a moment, Guydo continued. "Now I want you to tell me more of this place called Eden. I have heard tales of a group of people who teach of another God greater than Lucifer. I have no hope if Lucifer is all there is, for I am now his enemy, and there is no escaping his wrath in this life or the next."

"Let me speak, if I may," said Shadi. "I am of the Line of Light that the serpent worshipers have condemned as a subversive cult that must be eradicated. We are considered dangerous because we teach the truth about Lucifer, the fallen angel who has made himself to be a god. He has rebelled against the one true God, Elohim, and has led the human race into rebellion against Elohim as well. I am an eyewitness of this garden called Eden. I have seen the flaming sword that keeps all men from entering there. It is wielded by a mighty angel of the true God, Elohim. He is greater than any wicked father of the giants, the so-called 'men of renown.' My father is Irad, son of Enoch, a mighty holy man who walks close to Elohim. He has told us much of things to come, especially that Elohim will bring judgment on this wicked human race. There is a very old man, the great-great-great-great-great-grandfather of us all. As far as I know, he still lives but must hide from the wrath of Lucifer who wants to silence his testimony to the truth of the one true God. He and his wife, the mother of us all, lived in the garden for a time until Lucifer used a serpent to deceive them into rebelling against Elohim. They were forced from the garden, and since then, most of their offspring have lost touch with Elohim because of the lies of Lucifer. We Sethites and the Line of Light are dedicated to being the transmitters of the truth. We pass the truth on to each new generation so they will know that Elohim is the one true Creator of all things and that He loves and protects all who believe in Him alone."

Guydo was quiet as he reflected on this story, for it was his first time to hear it. He looked at Shadi and said, "My friend, this is a story that is too good to be true. Your chains and your scars make me want to believe you are sincere, for you have truly suffered much for what you believe."

"What I have suffered is nothing compared to the peace I always have in my heart because I know the truth," Shadi said softly. He could tell Guydo thirsted after his faith.

"I have lost all I have ever had in my search for the garden," said

Baqash when he saw Guydo deal with the possibility of the existence of a God of love who might also be a true concern for him.
"My loss of all becomes a waste to me unless I see this garden. I
must be free to continue my search for it."

"You men leave me no alternative. I cannot allow you to roam
freely here among us. I must keep you under guard, for your hearts
tell me that you will not stay here by your own choice. I will think
on these things. Then I will make my decision. I will either kill you,
or I will do as you have said and let you go in blindfolds." When
Guydo stood up, his hulking frame appeared dreadful. He called in
his men and gave them instructions. "Put these men in chains and
keep them under guard until I tell you what to do with them. Feed
them well and give them drink, but do not leave them alone for any
reason."

Baqash was having a hard time accepting this judgment
from Guydo as he sat with Shadi in their tent, once again bound
in chains. He began to second guess the way they had handled
this situation. Maybe they should have tried to escape while they
were unchained instead of trying to reason with Guydo. It would
have been better to die trying to escape than to be killed without
a chance to fight for their lives. All the pain and suffering he had
endured seemed senseless to him if it all was to end here in a cave.
The more he thought, the angrier he became.

Shadi spoke when he sensed that Baqash was struggling with
the situation. "Elohim will convince this man that we must continue
our journey."

"How can you be so sure? This man has a strong allegiance to his people. He will never jeopardize them. He owes us nothing, and we can be of no benefit to him. He has killed many other men for less reason than he has to kill us." Baqash was not in a mood to be encouraged.

"I have prayed to Elohim, the Keeper of men's hearts, who has the heart of even the high priest of Hellsrun in His hands. I have been given peace in my heart that He will deliver us from the hand of Guydo."

Baqash did not want to talk anymore. It was of no use to argue with this religious dreamer. He would not waste his time, for he did not feel he had that much to waste. He lay in silence, a twinge of hope flickering deep in his heart, hope that Shadi might be right after all. For some reason, Baqash had no answer for this situation. In the past he had always been able to fight his way out of tight spots, but this time he had lost the fight within himself. He lay restless in his chains all during the night, stirring in sleepless anticipation of what might come in the morning.

The guards came to take Baqash and Shadi to Guydo's dwelling. They were brought before him as he sat at table, finishing his morning meal. Guydo continued to eat as the men waited in front of him. With his mouth still full of food, he began to speak. "I did not sleep well last night. I had a recurring dream of the flaming sword of which you spoke. In my dream, I put you two men before it, intending to have it execute you. But when I did, it would do you no harm. Instead it slashed at me. Before I received a death blow, I woke up in much sweat and fear. My mind tells me you must die, but my heart loathes the thought. I have decided, against my better judgment, that you shall live. I want you to go and find this flaming sword and one day return to Krin. I will find you there, and you can take me to this garden."

As Guydo commanded the guards to loose his captives for their blindfolded journey out of the cave, Baqash was speechless. He could not believe what he had just heard. His mind raced as the remembered all his thoughts and fears of the night before.

The words of Shadi broke into his thoughts. "Guydo, you have been confronted with the very presence of almighty Elohim. You have shown your great wisdom by your willingness to listen to the very voice of God. By sparing us you have saved yourself from the hand of Elohim. You are a blessed man in a cursed world."

Guydo crossed the room to stand before Baqash and looked him in the eye. "I envy you, Baqash. I would give all I have to be released from the burden of the lives of these people so that I might go and search for what I have always felt in my heart is true. You must make a covenant with me to return. Promise me that you will report to me what you find."

Baqash, still stunned by what was taking place in his own hearing, looked at Guydo and said, "When I see the flaming sword, I will tell all who are willing to listen. You shall be one of many to hear my story." The two men shook hands, and Baqash and Shadi were led from Guydo's dwelling to prepare for their journey out of the cave.

Seventeen

A New Start in Krin

Blindfolds were put over the two men's eyes, and they were led from the cave, following a route that seemed to be different than the way in which they had been brought. They had become accustomed to the cave's structure by now and were familiar with its layout, even when wearing blindfolds. It did not matter to them how they were taken out of the cave, however; all that mattered was that they would soon be free men with new clothes, new boots for their feet, and plenty of coins and precious stones to help pay their way to the land of the Four Forks in the River.

They were taken to the edge of the forest where a rarely used road could be followed to lead them back to Krin. The trip to the road was long, and it was obvious that they were not taking a direct path. Their guides wanted to be sure they would not be able to retrace their steps. This was a much easier route to travel than the one they had taken coming in. Their chains were gone, their hands and feet were free, and they had no fear of being followed.

After several degrees' movement of the sun, they found themselves walking on what seemed to be a beaten path that was no longer covered in thick brush. This had to be the road they were to take to Krin. They walked several miles on the road before coming to a stop. It truly was impossible for Baqash or Shadi to know where to leave the road to return to the cave.

They were told to remove the blindfolds and then given instructions to keep following the road for several more miles to Krin. The leader of their guides gave them final words of warning. "I did not agree to letting you go. That was Guydo's decision. For some reason you have escaped the hands of death, but if the priests discover our cave because of you and I survive, I will find you and kill you myself. Now go and return here no more."

Baqash and Shadi walked down the road, away from the band of men, who stood and watched until the two travelers followed a bend in the road that took them out of sight. As they walked together, they were silent. Though they had experienced so much together, they had known each other for a very short time. They followed a back road toward the city where they had met in the prison wagon that was about to take them to their deaths in Hellsrun, and there was much to consider as they walked down the road to Krin as free men.

Baqash remembered his servant, Megado. He would not be able to order Shadi around as he had Megado. He was still amazed at how much the young slave had come to mean to him, and for the first time, he began to think about how Megado's untimely death was more a victory than a tragedy. It was much like what he remembered of the death of Adoniel, a release into something better. Baqash had never considered himself to be one who was afraid to die, for death had always been part of his warrior way of life. But now there was a yearning in his heart to have whatever it was that gave these men unexplainable peace even in the face of death. Baqash wanted to experience that kind of power. And now he would have his chance to possibly find it at the garden near the Four Forks in the River.

Baqash looked at Shadi in wonderment as they walked along together. Shadi had the look of one in deep meditation, one who was speaking silently with himself as though talking to another. Baqash had never met a man quite like him. He was so ugly with his scarred face and weathered skin, yet there was something about him that gave him a kind of glow. Baqash had just at this moment noticed that glow. It was a silent shining that showed most gently in his eyes. This was a man of slight stature who had, through much tribulation, grown strong within himself. Baqash realized that this man had found the power that he had begun to hunger for himself.

"And now I can finish my mission begun by the Lord through my cousin, Adoniel," said Shadi, breaking the silence. "My God Elohim has delivered us from the hands of death in order that you might find life, my friend."

The statement brought Baqash back to reality—and suspicion. "We have a long way to travel," he said. "Our journey is not yet over, and the serpent god, Lucifer, does not give up so easily. I will not believe he can be defeated until I see the garden and the flaming sword. Until then, I will do all I have to do to stay alive, just as I have always had to do." Although Baqash spoke defiantly in Shadi's hearing, he knew in his heart their deliverance from the cave was something he had nothing to do with.

Dusk was approaching as they looked down the road and saw

the lights of Krin beginning to dot the falling darkness. They would have to avoid checkpoints going into the city, but once in, they would be able to find food and lodging for the night. At the rising of the sun, they would purchase mounts for their journey to the land of the Four Forks in the River.

They were able to climb into the back of a wagon coming in from the fields. It was the time of evening when the city gates closed, and the guards were in a hurry to get off duty and head to a tavern. The wagon was not searched.

The two travelers found a place to stay close to the stables. They would buy two megalosaurs and head east on the Tropic of Cancer Highway as soon as the city gates reopened. They would then leave with a caravan so they could avoid the checkpoint. If they were thought to be guards of the caravan, they could leave the city with little chance of being discovered.

There was a tavern next to the lodge where Baqash and Shadi checked in, and they decided it would be a good place to find some food and drink. The room was loud with music, and the wine had been flowing for some time. They finally found a place to sit at a table in a corner, out of the way of the crowd. They wanted to stay unnoticed.

As they ate their bread and drank their wine, they became aware that they were being watched. Baqash and Shadi could see different men around the room eyeing them. A group of the men formed around their table, and one of them spoke up. "We ain't seen you men around here before. What brings you to Krin?"

"Baqash looked at Shadi and then back to his plate as he tore a piece of bread from the loaf. "You men want something from us?" he said slowly.

"You might say that, replied the spokesman. "You two men got something we want real bad. Bad enough to take it if we have to."

At that moment a long, shiny knife slammed its point into the middle of the table. The man holding the handle was unrecognizable in his hooded cape, but those standing in the group around the table knew who he was. They jumped back as the man said, "The first one of you who touches either of these men is a dead man." As he spoke, several men around the tavern stood to their feet with their hands ready to pull a knife or sword, and the group of men around the table began to slowly back away.

As they walked away, the man in the cape sat down at the table with Baqash and Shadi. It was Guydo. "I decided I had better keep an eye on you here in Krin until you got out of the city. It can be a dangerous place if you don't know what is going on. This tavern is a hangout for debased men who no longer desire women."

"I thought they looked at us strangely when we came in," said Shadi.

"They were not looking," said Guydo. "They were lusting. This kind of men would kill for a moment's pleasure, only to kill again."

"I saw many of those kind while in Hellsrun," said Baqash. "They respect nothing but what they desire for themselves. Once again we owe you our lives, Guydo."

"How do you plan to leave the city?" Guydo asked.

"Tomorrow at the coming of the sun, we will buy megalosaurs. Then we plan to pass as guards for a caravan leaving the city,"

Baqash replied.

"That sounds like a good plan. I will have some of my men stationed outside the city to ward off any guards who may try to pursue you if you are discovered. I will find you in Krin at the time you return," said Guydo.

Before the two men could respond, Guydo was gone. They watched him leave the tavern as other men followed him out into the darkness. They now knew that at least while they were in Krin, they had a few allies watching over them. It was a comforting thought as they returned to their lodging to rest until the rising of the sun.

The keeper of the stables had two megalosaurs with trappings. His asking price was high compared to what the animals usually cost. "That is a steep price for what we hope to get," said Shadi to the keeper.

"Let's just say there is a price to be paid to keep a man quiet when the serpent priests come calling," said the keeper. "I know a fugitive when I see one."

"Is there a caravan leaving the city today?" asked Baqash, showing no sign of concern about the keeper's intuition.

"There is a caravan leaving, but word is there will be a special watch for temple fugitives who do not carry the mark of the serpent. There have been reports that men who escaped from here in a stolen prison wagon not many rotations ago may be in the city," replied the keeper suspiciously. "My suggestion would be to go over the city wall and looks for these megalosaurs in the forest on the east side of the city. Guydo will have some men waiting there for you."

"How do we know this is not a trap?" asked Baqash, anger evident in his voice.

"It may be a trap, and then again, I guess it may not be. Seems to me you two men don't have much choice except to try your luck," said the keeper matter-of-factly. "I guess you'll just have to have a little faith in someone besides yourselves. There just may be something out there bigger than Lucifer himself. I guess we never know till we put the idea to a test. This may be that test for you."

The two men looked at each other, and Baqash asked Shadi, "What do you think?"

"I think Elohim oftentimes does things in strange ways. As the keeper says, we just have to have some faith."

Baqash could not believe he was actually willing to follow this risky scheme. It went against his distrustful nature. But something seemed to make the plan feel right. "All right," he said. "We will leave the megalosaurs here and go over the wall. We will pay you half now and half in the forest. Know this, stable keeper: if this is a trap, I will find a way to make you pay a higher price than you have required of us."

The two fugitives left the stable in search of a place to go over the city wall. The wall was high, but they found a point where a river ran next to the wall for several feet. The water was deep and crystal clear, a perfect place to jump when the time was right. Guards patrolled the wall, but when the guard changed, there was a window of time that was just long enough to make their escape, and that time came in the next degree of the sun.

When the moment was right, Baqash and Shadi made their move. They came out from behind a corner where they were hiding and ran for the edge of the wall. Baqash had noticed that his companion was acting nervous, but he thought nothing of it until they leapt from the wall into a dead run. Shadi could not contain himself, "Elohim, have mercy!" he cried as they flew into the air over the river below.

Baqash realized in that instant that Shadi, for all his faith, did not know how to swim. He knew the moment they hit the water he would have to pull Shadi to safety. And there was a problem. The guards had heard Shadi's cry during the changing of the guard, for they had run to the edge of the wall to see what was happening. Now Baqash had only one choice. When they hit the water, he went under and grabbed Shadi's collar, dragging him to the surface. The moment their heads broke the water, Baqash slugged Shadi to knock him unconscious. He knew this was the only way he could get control of him quickly.

Baqash did not try to swim to the bank of the river across from where the guards had come to look for them from the top of the wall. He swam down river, which led away from the wall and then headed to a clump of bushes overhanging the riverbank. He climbed from the river into the bushes as the guards attempted shots at them with their bows. They went down river far enough to be out of range for even the best of archers, and Baqash pulled Shadi from the water just as he began to regain consciousness.

"Wake up!" Baqash yelled at Shadi. "We have no time to waste! The guards will have the whole city on alert. We have to get out of here."

Shadi shook his head, struggling to come to his senses. Stumbling to his feet, he followed Baqash's lead into the thick growth of the forest. His composure returned as they ran through the trees. Now they wondered where they would find the men with the megalosaurs. As they ran, they heard a loud whistle from above. They looked up to see a man waving them over to his location.

The time had come to see if their trust had been well placed, but when they got to the tree where they had seen the man, something strange happened. The two megalosaurs were there, saddled and waiting, but no one was with them. The man in the tree was nowhere to be found, and nobody was there to take the rest of the money they owed the stable keeper.

This was strange, but the men had no time to waste looking for anyone. They mounted the megalosaurs and headed deeper into the forest, leaving Krin far behind. They knew the guards would have to get organized to track them, and by then they planned to be well on their way to the land of the Four Forks in the River.

On and one they rode until they reached a clearing. They decided to head north, following the edge of the forest until they came to a road that would take them east again. After several miles, they came to a wagon trail going the direction they wanted. They followed it for many hours, riding into the night. From what Baqash could remember of the maps he had seen, the land north and east of Krin was sparsely populated with many forests and prairies that led to low-lying hills bordering the land of the secret garden called Eden.

As they entered another forest covering, they realized it would be too dark to continue to ride. The tall, dense trees would block out the bright reflection of the moon, so the two men halted in the forest and made camp for the rest of the night. As they were setting up, Baqash opened a saddle bag to see what might be in it that they could use. Much to his surprise, the money they had paid for the megalosaurs was in the saddlebags.

Baqash and Shadi were puzzled by the money as they settled down to sleep. Who was the stable keeper anyway? How did he seem to know so much about them? He had to have had more than a hunch bout them. Was this a trap that was still playing itself out? Maybe something had happened to make the trap fail, or perhaps this was Guydo's work. He certainly seemed to have a lot of connections in the underground community at Krin. But how could it be Guydo? He had told them he would help them escape if they were caught in a caravan search. His men would have been waiting in a different place close to the city gate, which was a good distance from where they went over the wall.

"Elohim works in strange ways," said Shadi. "My grandfather, Enoch, is a man who lives so close to Elohim that some believe one day he will be taken into the skies in a gust of flaming fire. He is a prophet who speaks of many things to come. He named my uncle *Methuselah*, which means that when my uncle dies, Elohim will bring a great judgment upon this world and those who worship Lucifer. He has spoken many things that have already come to pass, and he himself had prophesied that Elohim will take him to Himself without suffering death. Adoniel was the one who told me these things. Enoch also spoke of how there are servant angels of Elohim who are sent by Him to give aid or protection to those who are doing His work in the world."

"Where were these so-called angels when Adoniel died in the arena at Hellsrun? Where were these helpers when Megado took that spear in his side?" asked Baqash, unimpressed by Shadi's suggested explanation of the unusual events of the day. "All I know is that you almost got us both killed in the river this day. If I had not pulled you out, you would have had an arrow in you or you would be in another prison wagon headed for Hellsrun right now."

"Yes, I was foolish not to say something about my fear of water, but going over the wall was our only hope, so I just left us both in the hands of Elohim. I give Him thanks for the strength He gave to you to bring us both to safety, even though my jaw is still smarting from your blow to my chin," replied Shadi, rubbing his sore jaw.

"That is something I do not yet understand about what is happening to me," said Baqash. "Before I started this whole senseless quest, I was the kind of man who would have let you drown in the river and saved myself. Something is happening to me that I can't explain. I guess I realized that you are my only real hope to lead me to the garden. If the garden is not as you say, I believe I will run a sword through you and go back to Hellsrun to receive the mark of the serpent."

"I think what we need is some sleep before the morning light," said Shadi in a controlled, quiet voice. "We have had a great struggle, and there is much left to come. Rest has a way of calming an angry soul."

The two men lay down to rest, but it was some time before Baqash could sleep. Questions filled his mind about Enoch, servant angels, coming judgment, and this God, Elohim. Baqash felt an urge to want to believe, but there were so many questions that filled his heart with doubt. He had to see this garden called Eden for himself.

Eighteen

Koah

The two men awoke to the sound of an animal making cries of distress. The megalosaurs jostled nervously at the sound. They had moved off the wagon path, several steps into the thicket, to set up camp because they did not want to be seen by any possible passersby while they slept. The cries came from deeper in the forest.

They got up and looked for edible plants to fill their bellies. They found nuts, berries, and some roots that they could eat. Streams of water were abundant in the forest where they could wash themselves and their food. During their search, the cries continued, and forest creatures ran by, spooked by the sound. A deer, an elk, a rabbit, and even a stegosaurus came by with two of its young following.

Baqash decided to try to discover the source of the distressed sound while Shadi stayed with the megalosaurs at the camp. As he neared the roaring cries, he noticed large tracks of a three-clawed, two-footed animal. There seemed to be several animals together, and Baqash knew that behemoths often ran in packs. However, this did not concern him because the animals were not a threat to humans unless taught by man to become bloodthirsty killers, for they normally fed on the leaves and berries of trees.

The cries were coming from a pit in a clearing Baqash came upon. Tracks were everywhere, as if there had been a scuffle, and he noticed several human tracks in the midst of the pit. Looking in, he saw a dead female behemoth with several spear wounds in its side. Crouching next to it was a yearling male behemoth, mourning over the dead body of its mother.

This was a strange sight. Usually behemoth hunters killed a mother and took its young to be sold as killer behemoth trainees for the temple arenas. When Baqash jumped into the pit to try to calm the young animal, he learned why the hunters had left it there to die: it had broken a leg during the fall into the pit with its mother. The hunters would not have wanted to take the time to splint the leg and let it heal. There were enough healthy behemoths in the forests of the world to not want to worry with this one.

As he looked at the helpless animal, something happened inside Baqash, and that something would not allow him to leave the young behemoth there to die. He felt he had to do what he could to help the doomed beast. After calming the animal with soothing words and soft strokes of his hand, he climbed out of the pit. But when he did, the yearling began to cry out again.

Baqash ran back to the camp where Shadi was waiting with the megalosaurs. "Untie the animals! I need them to help us save a yearling behemoth that is dying in a pit."

Shadi was speechless. This man who had said he would kill him the night before was now trying to save a dying animal. He could only go along with what was happening and hope to understand later. Baqash's excitement told Shadi to move quickly to release the animals he had already saddled for their journey, a journey now put on hold. They hurried back to where Baqash has found his orphaned child.

"Help me find some sleeping plants. We will need to sedate the animal first," said Baqash as they reached the side of the pit where the behemoth still cried in pain. Holding the reins of his megalosaur, Shadi looked over the edge of the pit to see what had trapped Baqash in the grip of compassion. He tied his animal to a tree and looked for the fernlike plants with special sedative qualities.

"Here! Over here are some sleeping plants!" yelled Baqash. "Help me gather enough to put the behemoth to sleep."

"We'll have to force-feed it," said Shadi as he ran to help Baqash. Shadi was beginning to feel the excitement of the challenge of saving the helpless beast. The skills he had developed as a shepherd for saving his sheep burned in his heart once again. How ironic the situation seemed! Here they were, a couple of hunted men running for their lives, trying to save the life of an animal, but it seemed that this was the right thing to do.

They did not worry about the possibility of the hunters coming back. Those men were already somewhere else, caught up in trying to trap other animals they could sell to become bloodthirsty killers. Trying to help this one animal was a way of protesting against the savage acts of men. Baqash could still remember his days in the training fortress of the Violent Ones. The vicious way trainers had slaves killed and their blood fed to the young behemoths was still vivid in his mind. The beasts soon learned how to kill the slaves themselves in order to get the sweet taste of blood they had been taught to crave. Baqash was determined that this was one behemoth that would not develop that craving.

The two men force-fed the beast that, for its age, was already quite large. It was as tall as a man and growing fast, as did all behemoths. It weighed several hundred more pounds than a man as well. It was not an easy task, but the huge child finally went to sleep. Then it was all the men could do to pull the broken leg into a set position. Once that was done, they put tree branches on the leg and tied it with cords stripped from other branches.

Once the leg was set, they knocked down a side of the pit to create a slope to allow them to drag the animal out of it. They slid the ends of two poles under their patient and tied the other ends to make a *V*. Next they put two cross poles under the behemoth and tied them to the long V-shaped poles. Laying the *V* section of the poles over the back of one of the megalosaurs, they tied it to the saddle. The four poles became a bed for the behemoth to lie on while being dragged behind the megalosaur. They could travel like this for a few days until the broken leg had mended. Broken bones mended very quickly in those days, especially the bones of a young, fast-growing behemoth. Once it was strong again, they would set their new pet free.

"What should we call the animal?" asked Baqash as they left the pit and returned to the wagon trail, dragging the behemoth behind them.

"I don't know," replied Shadi, realizing that giving this animal a name was Baqash's right as the one who had chosen to save it. "What do you think its name should be?"

"It is going to be very large and very strong someday. We should name it Koah. Yes, that is it. We shall call the animal *Koah*."

Baqash rode the megalosaur that was dragging Koah, and Shadi rode alongside as they continued east down the wagon trail through the forest. They stopped fairly often to feed Koah and give it water since they no longer were concerned about those who pursued them from Krin. They would have given up the search by now, even if they had been able to pick up their trail. Whoever had had the megalosaurs waiting had done them a great service. The thought of how all that had taken place came to their minds often as they rode side by side. Who was that stable keeper? What happened to the man who had whistled from the tree? Shadi was convinced that Elohim had sent some angels; Baqash felt it all had to be the work of Guydo.

After two rotations, Koah was becoming restless. The broken leg looked as if it were strong enough to hold the young animal's weight again, so they slowly removed the splint after taking down the V-shaped poles and laid them down so that Koah could get up on its feet from level ground. As soon as the behemoth was on the ground, it rolled into position to stand up. It moved quickly to its feet, walking around with a limp, not yet willing to put full weight on the injured leg. It would take another rotation before it would no longer favor its leg.

The two men thought their project would run into the forest now that it was free from the splint and able to run again. But that wasn't the case. When they mounted their megalosaurs and began to ride away, Koah followed them, crying as it had when Baqash had found it with its slain mother. It became apparent to them that Koah was still too young to be on its own, and now they were its only mother figure. Koah was here to stay, at least for now anyway.

They journeyed northeast, following the stars and staying on back roads and trails that led in the direction they wanted to go. All along the way their pet behemoth followed not far behind. The scenery was changing as they traveled. They were passing through low-lying mountains and hills that were full of waterfalls that fed several streams that watered the lush, tropical vegetation of a rainforest without the rain. The forest was full of birds of all colors, shapes, and sizes. They called out to each other in the trees. The travelers also saw many kinds of monkeys, squirrels, and raccoons running in the trees as they rode beneath them. They chattered and squealed at the intruders who had invaded their domain.

The place was teeming with all kinds of animal life, large and small. They rode by a lake where a herd of duckbilled dinosaurs grazed on the underwater plants. Hippopotamuses yawned near the banks while alligators cruised the lake, eating water lilies. Once a striped tiger left the woods to get a drink. All these animals lived off the land in harmony. It was a sad thing that man could not live in that same harmony like the animals around him.

Shadi told Baqash that this new terrain was a good sign, for there was a low-rising mountain range that ran north to south just west of the valley where the Four Forks in the River lay. He was sure this was that mountain range. He felt they would reach their destination in a few more rotations. It was good news to Baqash. He was ready to see if what he had been hearing was true. He was also ready to see if all that he had been through would be rewarded with truth or a lie.

It had been several rotations since they had set Koah free from its splint. They had not ridden quickly, nor had they moved too slowly, but they had kept a good pace, stopping only to feed the animals and take an occasional drink of cool water from the streams that were fed by underground springs. Baqash and Shadi continued to eat the berries, leafy plants, and roots they found. All the while they avoided any signs of man. They stayed away from small towns and villages, and they did not stop to talk at any of the remote houses they encountered. They just kept moving toward their destination.

Shadi knew they were close to his home, but he did not know how close. It was time to stop and ask how near they were to the valley of the Four Forks in the River. They decided to inquire at a small village they came upon in the forest. There was not a temple or any temple priests there to check them for the mark of the serpent. They would stop, ask directions, and hope not to draw too much attention to themselves.

Baqash decided it would be better to go into the village alone. "Stay here with the animals, and I will walk into the village to learn where we are," he said as they rode to the side of a clearing where smoke rose from a few small huts made from materials from the forest that surrounded them.

"Be careful," warned Shadi. "Some of the people in these parts are bandits. I have been attacked more than once by small bands of thieves while shepherding my sheep. They ride in, steal two or three sheep, and then ride off. Sometimes those shepherds who tried to chase them down were ambushed and ended up dead if they were not careful."

As he walked into the middle of the group of huts, which encircled a fire pit, Baqash became more and more uneasy. There was no stirring or movement of any kind, and it seemed far too quiet for this time of day. Suddenly men ran from the huts in all directions, wielding weapons and screaming like crazed animals. It was an ambush. Shadi's fears were confirmed, for Baqash had walked into a village of bloodthirsty thieves.

Grabbing his weapon, Baqash ran toward what seemed to be the weakest point in the circle of thieves running toward him. He managed to break through a seam, knocking down two men with quick, lethal blows. They were obviously untrained and clumsy foes. He headed for an escape route, hoping Shadi would meet him with the megalosaurs before his pursuers could catch him.

What happened next caught Baqash and the trail of thieves behind him totally by surprise. As the men from the village chased Baqash, yelling and screaming, a fierce roar emerged from the forest and ran directly at the men. Baqash headed for the shelter of the forest as Koah burst past him, heading straight toward the group of now-confused bandits. The huge tail-throwing, leg-stomping behemoth was far more than they had bargained for. Those who could began to run in all directions to avoid the fierce encounter with this huge, angry beast. The others were either sent sprawling by blows from Koah's tail, which was the size of a cedar tree, or kicks from its taloned feet, which were almost as big as the men they sent flying through the air.

Baqash stopped running and watched in amazement as Koah turned the pursuers into a mass of frantic cowards trying to find a way of escape. Baqash and Shadi had not seen Koah for several rotations and certainly did not realize it had the capacity to be this violent without having been trained by man for it. It had become like a dog that was always ready to save its master. Koah must have been in the forest nearby, watching all along. What a great friend to have at a time such as this!

Shadi rode up, laughing, and stopped to pick up Baqash. They quickly rode away before the dispersed thugs could gather their courage and try a counter attack. As Baqash mounted his megalosaur, he called out to Koah to follow, and they rode off into the forest with their deliverer not far behind.

Nineteen

A Mysterious Old Man

The travelers continued on a trail that brought them over the low-lying mountain range and then into a valley of green, rolling hills covered with lush grasses and clumps of brilliant flowers. A large river flowed peacefully through the bends created by the position of the hills. As Shadi saw the river, he stopped his megalosaur and dismounted. He fell to his knees and bowed his head to the ground, weeping silent tears of joy and saying, "Bless the Lord Elohim! Bless the Lord Elohim!"

"What is wrong with you?" asked Baqash gruffly as he wheeled around to see why Shadi had stopped and dismounted so abruptly.

"I had to stop and give thanks to Elohim, for I never thought I would see my home again! This is the first of the four rivers that flow from the river of Eden called Pishon. We can follow it north, and it will take us to the land of the Four Forks in the River," replied Shadi, his voice still shaking with tears.

Baqash said no more. He sat silently in his saddle, waiting for Shadi to finish this solemn, genuine act of worship to his God. It made Baqash wonder if he would ever see his home again. And if he did, would anyone rejoice to see him? Would Landua still reject him for his rebellion against Lucifer? The thoughts and memories brought a new sense of despair to his heart. Was all that he had been through really worth the hurt and pain he had brought on himself and those he loved the most?

After a short period, Shadi rose and mounted his megalosaur. By this time Koah had run up to see what was happening, like a young, curious boy. After the incident at the forest village, Koah didn't wander off as far as it had before. As the men turned the animals to head north up the Pishon River, Shadi looked over at Koah and said, "Koah, let's go home." The young behemoth raised its large head with a gesture that seemed to nod in agreement and gave a long hiss as if to say, "Yes, let's go home."

The threesome traveled north, following the river for three rotations. Shadi spoke almost constantly now. He was excited to see the many familiar landmarks he had learned while traveling with his family, moving from grazing pasture to grazing pasture with their sheep, all the while trying to avoid the temple priests of the serpent who hunted them relentlessly. He told story after story of things that had happened as he was reminded of them by the places he saw. It impressed Baqash that a lowly shepherd could have such a rich and meaningful life despite all the hardships. It seemed that it was Shadi's faith in his Elohim that made the difference.

The roar of rushing water grew louder and louder in the distance. As the travelers came over the rise of a large, rolling hill, Baqash was overcome by one of the most beautiful sights he had ever seen. A wide, roaring river spilled over low misting waterfalls into a clear, smooth lake that looked like blue-tinted glass. They were overlooking the mouth of the Pishon as they stopped to see the sight of the lake in all its glory.

"The other three rivers begin to the east of here, flowing out of the lake. The lake is fed by the river from Eden as well as underground springs, and that is why all four rivers are large rivers as well. They have a bountiful source of water flowing from the innermost part of the earth. We call it the fountain of the great deep," said Shadi as they gazed at the sights.

"How can we find your people if they move so often from place to place?" asked Baqash as he began to refocus on the journey at hand.

"There will be signs," Shadi replied confidently. "I'm sure my people will find us before we find them. They have learned not to be taken by surprise. They keep an eye out for all who come and go."

They decided to make camp on the hill overlooking the falls and the lake. The sound of the roaring falls would provide a pleasant background to their sleep that night. The next day they would begin their search for Shadi's shepherd family in the hills farther north, upriver from the lake. Shadi knew of some special hideaways they could possibly be using during this constellation in the revolution around the sun.

It was early the next morning, before the sun's appearing, when the two made preparations to begin their search. Baqash felt somewhat excited about the possibility that this story of Eden might be true. The beauty of what he had already seen gave him a sense of hope in his heart.

As they took off on their search for Shadi's people, Koah ran

ahead, stopping and sniffing as it went, looking over the new terrain. The behemoth disappeared over a hill and then reappeared on
the other side. Periodically it returned to the two men to reassure
itself that all was well; then it would take off again. This went on for
several degrees as the sun moved toward the middle of the sky.

After a period of time, Baqash noticed that Koah had not returned or come into sight in quite a while, and he began to wonder
if something had gone wrong. Maybe Koah had found something,
or maybe it was in trouble of some kind. Maybe it had decided
it was time to go out on its own. The animal had certainly grown
stronger and much larger in the last several moons since they
had found it in the pit with its dead mother. Whatever the reason,
Baqash decided it might not be a bad idea to try to find Koah.

"I haven't seen Koah in a while," Baqash said to Shadi as they
rode alongside the river on a dusty, sheep-worn path. "I think we
ought to try to find the beast. Maybe it has turned up something
that might be a help to us."

Shadi agreed, and they took off in the direction where they had
last seen Koah. They went up into the rocky hills some distance
away from the river valley. As they crossed over the second hill, they
heard singing. The two men stopped to listen for a moment, and
Shadi's face erupted into a broad smile. A strange feeling came over
Baqash, as if he had heard a song like this once before. Shadi yelped
with joy and ran over the hill while Baqash sat on his mount, still
trying to recognize the song.

Spurring his megalosaur, he took off after Shadi, realizing his
companion knew exactly where he was headed. When he topped

the hill, the sight he saw was very disturbing. A flock of sheep huddled on one side of a green pasture, next to a clump of rocks. Koah lay on the green grass of the pasture, mesmerized by the singing. Shadi was laughing and hugging the shepherd of the sheep as if he was a long-lost brother. At that moment it all came back to him: Baqash had heard Adoniel sing a similar song to the killer behemoth in the arena at Hellsrun. *This shepherd,* he thought, drawing closer, *must be part of Shadi's family.*

As Baqash neared the two laughing and hugging men, he could see the family resemblance between them. He stopped his megalosaur and dismounted, waiting until the two shepherds finished their greetings. He knew Shadi would introduce him when he was ready. Their happiness and joy put a smile on his face as he watched their excited reunion.

"We thought you were already dead in Hellsrun," said the stranger, tears flowing from his eyes. "Dago returned to us and told us of Adoniel. We thought you had endured a similar death for our Lord Elohim."

"No, my cousin," laughed Shadi. "The Lord spared me for another very important task. He gave me the guardianship of a seeker of the truth to bring here to be with us. Elohim has, by His great mercies, chosen to reveal Himself to my friend who helped me escape from the hand of that serpent, Lucifer."

Shadi looked at Baqash and motioned for him to draw near. "Baqash," he said, smiling with a brightness in his eyes that was heightened by tears of joy, "I want you to meet my cousin, the older brother of Adoniel and the son of Methuselah. This is Lamech."

Baqash bowed slightly and acknowledged Shadi's introduction without showing too much weakness or loss of position as a warrior presented to a shepherd.

"Lamech, I want to introduce you to my warrior friend, my deliverer by the hand of Elohim, Baqash."

When Lamech heard the name, he stared at Baqash for a moment. Walking up to him and looking him squarely in the eye, he asked, "Are you the same Baqash who helped our Dago escape from the arena in Hellsrun?"

"I am the same," replied Baqash slowly, a little intimidated by this man who was being so forward.

Lamech fell to one knee and kissed Baqash's hand. "My family and I have said many prayers for you, and now I see the answer to our prayers standing here before me. Welcome, my friend, in the name of our Lord Elohim." Standing to his feet, he looked at Shadi and continued, "You must come with me. We will have a celebration unto the Lord. Our whole family will want to join us in this great expression of the power of our God."

Power of our God? Baqash thought. *The only power I have seen so far is my own power to stay alive.*

By this time Koah had begun to emerge from his stupor. He had wandered into the pasture where Lamech was tending his sheep. Thinking Koah might be a threat to his sheep by trying to play with them too roughly, Lamech had used the same singing that Adoniel had used.

They left the sheep and went deeper into the rocky hills to where the shepherd family had pitched their tents. Lamech sent one of the young boys to go and tend the sheep as he told the story of Baqash and Shadi's arrival. There was great excitement in the camp as they heard of Shadi's return and the presence of the hero warrior, Baqash. Dago was no longer living at this camp; he had married into another of the families nearby, so messengers were sent to tell him to come to the celebration. Other messengers were dispatched to call Shadi's family as well. The families stayed dispersed in small separate groups, a few degrees' journey apart. Lamech lived with his father, Methuselah, in this central camp where the chief patriarch of the clan lived. The women began bustling about, preparing the feast for the celebration.

Lamech took Shadi and Baqash to Methuselah's tent to rest and to clean up from their journey. They stayed in Lamech's quarters, for like Baqash and Shadi, he had not yet established his own household by marriage. Lamech gave his guests new garments, made by the women in the camp, to replace the tattered worn clothing they had worn since their escape from Krin. As Baqash removed the worn-out clothing, he saw himself in a mirror and noticed the faint scars from the chains he had worn in the captivity of the temple priests. He had come a long way in distance but even more so in the changes he had undergone as a person. The once feared and respected warrior now wore the clothes of a lowly shepherd and stayed in a tent with nothing of his own to call family or home.

After allowing a time of rest, Lamech entered his quarters to give the men a message. "The feast is almost ready," he said. "Dago and your family, Shadi, should be here soon." He paused and became serious. In a reverential tone he continued. "My father has spoken to the Old and Wise One and told him of your arrival. He has become weak in his nine hundred twenty-nine revolutions around the sun and will not come to the celebration. But he desires to see you in the next dawn of the morning light. I will come and take you to meet him then. I will get word to you when the others have come. Then the feast will begin!"

After Lamech left the room, Baqash turned to Shadi and asked, "Who is the Old and Wise One he speaks of?"

Shadi became serious as Lamech had. "I have spoken little of him until now because each of us in our clan is bound by oath not to mention him to anyone outside our families. Many revolutions ago, the high priest of the serpent tried to silence him, for he is the father of us all, and his story is a great threat to the serpent god, Lucifer. He is the main reason the temple priests hunted us so fervently in the past, and he is the cause of much fear in them. We put out a story among the towns and villages in the valley that he is already dead, in hopes that the priests will not pursue us as strongly as they have in the past. The plan has helped, for the persecution has calmed some since that time. But if the high priest were to get word of his existence among us, he would become as relentless in his search for the Old and Wise One as before."

This new information about a mysterious old man raised a lot of questions in Baqash's mind. "When you say he is the father of us all, you mean he is the oldest of your clan, correct?"

"No, that is not what I mean at all. What I mean is he is the first man created by our great Creator, Elohim. All of humanity are descendants of his seed. He is your father as well."

Although he tried not to show it, this information was still as outrageous to Baqash as it had been when Adoniel first mentioned it. It was so different from all he had ever been told. It had always seemed natural to him that animals and men had developed out of lesser kinds of animals and that animals and man were kindred to each other. He had never accepted that Lucifer was the god of the process, for it seemed more reasonable to him that it had all just happened on its own. The earth, sun, moon, planets, and stars had always been in existence until something—a small, out-of-the-way beginning—happened to get living things started. The religion of the serpent was too bloody and ugly to have had anything to do with the beauty of the earth he saw everywhere. Maybe this Elohim was the God who had made it happen, but how could all mankind have one father? The idea was more than Baqash could comprehend.

"You seem to be disturbed by what I have told you about the Old and Wise One," said Shadi. "It may seem hard to accept at this time, but when you meet him, you will come to see that what I say about him is true. Elohim will enlighten your understanding to the truth of these things."

Baqash stayed in the tent and waited for the feast to begin. Shadi went out into the camp to visit with his relatives and catch up on what had happened since he had been stolen away so long ago. Baqash was now even more intrigued by all that had happened to him. These shepherd people were not like any he had ever encountered before—first Adoniel, then Shadi, and now men like Lamech and this Old and Wise One. It was as though they lived in a completely different world from the one he had always known. He had to admit to himself that he envied much of what their world had to offer. It was a much simpler and more caring kind of place.

A young boy soon came to tell Baqash that the guests from the other camps had arrived, and Baqash left the tent to go out and meet them. It was a large band of people—men, women, children, old and young alike. He recognized Dago from a distance as he worked to help a woman and her child dismount from a donkey they had ridden. Shadi was already in the arms of his parents and brothers and sisters, hugging, laughing, kissing, and crying tears of greater joy than all those before. Dago saw Baqash as he and his wife followed the group to the center of the camp. He said something to her; she nodded in agreement, and he hurried to greet the man whom Elohim had used to give him a new life. Dago was a huge, powerful man, but he ran to Baqash without hesitation, grabbing him in an embrace that only a stout man could endure. Then he held Baqash at arm's length so they could look at each other eye to eye and remember their first encounter. For a moment there was nothing to be said; their presence together said it all.

The feast was on. Music began to play, and dancing commenced. There were introductions, food and drink, more dancing, and many stories told all through the night. Dago told of his escape from the arena. Shadi told of his escape from the prison wagon with Baqash and Megado. The group finally convinced Baqash to tell of how he had met Adoniel and seen his triumphant death in the arena at Hellsrun. The story brought a hush and a sense of awe at the courageous stand of their Adoniel for his Lord Elohim. Then the group sang a song of praise that moved them back into the celebration, which was filled with music, dancing, and laughter. It was a time that no one there would soon forget.

Late in the night, Baqash checked on Koah and the megalosaurs. They were tied to stakes outside the camp. He wanted to make sure they had plenty to eat, but they were already well cared for. He then returned to Lamech's quarters in the tent of Methuselah. He wanted to get some rest before his meeting with the mysterious Old and Wise One, the man Shadi claimed to be the father of all men. The idea was still more than Baqash could comprehend, let alone believe. But there was deeper reason for leaving the celebration before the others: in the midst of the celebration, he remembered that only Shadi had come home. The thought made Baqash want to be alone.

Twenty

A Meeting with the Truth

There was lamplight burning in the room when Lamech awakened Baqash. "The morning light is about to break," he said softly, not wanting to startle his guest. "The women have prepared food for us to eat before we meet with the Old and Wise One. I will wait for you and Shadi outside."

Lamech left while Baqash struggled to get the sleep out of his head. He had not slept that deeply or peacefully since he left his father's house the first time to make his trip to Hellsrun. Shadi was still sound asleep. He had not finished celebrating until several degrees after Baqash had returned to the tent, and Baqash had not heard him when he came in. He decided to let Shadi sleep. It would be good for him to get his rest. Baqash pulled the shepherd's garment over his head and tied the sheepskin sandals on his feet. He was ready to meet the Old and Wise One.

Baqash ate bread cakes and drank hot herb tea with Lamech, seated on woolen rugs close to the cooking pots and the baking ovens. The women gave them the cakes hot from the oven, and melted goat butter dripped from the cakes as they ate them. It was quite a treat for a man who had not eaten a regular meal in many full moons.

"How old are you, Lamech?" asked Baqash. "It seems to me that you are close to my age."

"I am fifty-five revolutions around the sun. Still very young with very much to learn."

"So you are close to my age," replied Baqash. "What about a woman? Has your family made arrangements for you yet?"

"No, there is plenty of time for that. In our clan we do not move into such an important step too quickly. We want to be sure that a marriage bond will last a lifetime. If Elohim wills, I will live many more revolutions like my forefathers, and there will be plenty of children and children's children to come. The Old and Wise One had thirty children of his own, and many of his children have had more than he. I am the oldest of fifteen brothers and sisters, and I am sure my parents have more of them to come. We take very seriously Elohim's command to be fruitful and multiply and fill the earth."

As they continued eating their morning meal, a man emerged from an older,larger tent, not too far from where they were sitting. "Here comes my father from the tent of meeting," said Lamech, gesturing toward the tent from which his father had come. "It is where the Old and Wise One now lives his life before Elohim. My forefathers must be ready for the meeting."

"Your forefathers?" questioned Baqash in surprise. "I thought I was meeting with the Old and Wise One."

"You are," replied Lamech, smiling. "The Old and Wise One is the oldest of my forefathers. He is the chief of the council of our clan. Today we will meet with him and the rest of the clan council."

At that moment Methuselah came to where they sat. He was a tall, heavily bearded, soft-spoken man. Baqash could see the family resemblance between this man and his gallant son, Adoniel.

"Come, my sons," he said quietly. "The Old and Wise One is ready to meet our guest."

Without another word Methuselah turned and walked back to the old tent. The two young men rose and followed after him in silence. It was time to enter the presence of a person this clan of shepherds considered to be a holy man. Talking was no longer the acceptable thing to do. When they reached the tent door, Lamech stepped ahead of his father and threw open the flap of goat skins. Methuselah entered first, then Baqash, and finally Lamech followed, letting the goatskin flap fall back to its place.

In this large tent of meeting all the side flaps were pulled down. It was dimly lit with oil lamp stands encircling the room. Animal hides covered the floor, making a soft, soundless carpet to walk on. A circle of seven men sat at the front of the tent, on a platform elevated slightly above the floor. All the men were dressed as shepherds, and each looked ready to tend his flock. Some of the men were much older than the others, and some did not look old at all.

It was obvious, though, who the Old and Wise One was. He appeared much older than the rest, and all the men sat in facing him. No one was talking, and silence reigned as they waited for their guest to arrive. Baqash felt a little intimidated by the council of men. He had sat in councils with his father's leaders in Cainogan, but there was a presence in this place he had never felt before. Something was in the room that seemed greater than the men themselves.

As they crossed the large room, walking on the goat skins, Baqash could see the old man more clearly. His head was covered with a wool shawl, but his thin white hair protruded somewhat. His shoulders were stooped, his skin showed many years of wear, and his face was thin and drawn. But it was obvious that he had once been a strong, virile man. This was also a man whose hands and face showed that he had worked hard most of his days and who had suffered much pain and sorrow in his life. He looked serious as he sat before these men, gazing intently at Baqash as he and the other two men approached him.

When they reached the edge of the platform, Methuselah went directly to his place and sat down. Lamech took the seat next to his father. Baqash was left standing next to the platform, facing the Old and Wise One—outside the circle and not knowing what to do next. He felt awkward but decided the best thing would be to just stand and wait. The old man never took his eyes off Baqash. He merely sat, looking intently at his guest.

"Welcome, my son, to the Line of Light," said the old man, his voice weak and shaky but his face displaying a faint smile of approval. "My name is Adam, the name given me by my Creator, Elohim, for He called me Adam, the first man that He made in His image. These are the sons of nine generations that Elohim has given me in my image. They have proven themselves to be Elohim's choice to carry the light of His word for their generation. They are Seth, the son of Adam; Enosh, the son of Seth; Kenan, the son of Enosh; Kenan, the son of Enosh; Mahalelel, the son of Kenan; Jared, the son of Mahalelel; Enoch, the son of Jared; Methuselah, the son of Enoch; and Lamech, the son of Methuselah, whom Elohim will bless with a son in His time."

Baqash looked at each man in turn, wondering how the group had managed to stay together as a family all these years. Most of the families he knew were divided by greed and war before many generations had come.

"Come, my son, and sit here before me," the old man continued, motioning to Baqash to take a seat in the middle of the circle. Baqash reverently took his seat as Adam, the Old and Wise One, continued to speak. "I have been told that you are a seeker of the truth and have endured much hardship to make your way here to us. I do not believe that you will be disappointed, for Elohim has put it in my heart that He has chosen to reveal Himself to you. It matters not if you see the garden from which my wife and I were driven eight hundred thirty revolutions ago. For no man can truly believe in Elohim unless He chooses to reveal Himself to that man. But Elohim is always ready to show Himself to those who hunger to know the truth, for He Himself is the truth. There is no other."

Somehow Baqash knew that he was having an encounter that many people on the earth could only dream of in the secrets of their own hearts. Oh, to learn that there truly is something greater in life than what the serpent god, Lucifer, had given! There was a growing cry, deep within his heart, that longed to know that what he was experiencing was really true.

Next to the seat on which the Old and Wise One sat was a wooden box covered with pure gold. Adam opened the lid of the box and lifted out two large clay tablets, which were wrapped in thick wool blankets for protection. He took them out very carefully and unwrapped them one at a time, handling them as tenderly as a mother would her first newborn child when taking from his crib to cradle him in her arms. He looked at the tablets and stroked them as though they were his greatest possession. The nine men in the circle bowed their heads to the floor in humble adoration as they saw each unwrapped tablet. Baqash could tell that they were a central object of these men's faith, and he wondered what it was that made them so important.

As the sons of Adam rose from their bows, their patriarch spoke once again, turning his attention back to Baqash and looking him directly in the eye. "These two tablets are without price on this earth. They are my greatest responsibility as the protector of the truth. When my body has returned to dust and my soul has gone to its resting place to await its final deliverance, they will be passed down to these sons in the Line of Light as they each, in turn, become the protector of the truth.

"After my Creator formed me from the dust of the ground, he gave my wife to me as my perfect mate, taken from the side of my own flesh. He also formed these tablets from the same dust of the ground from which He had formed me. He wrote these words on the tablets with His own hand, for my keeping; they tell of how He created all things. As I lived in the garden with my wife, Elohim came in the cool of the evenings to teach us how to read the tablets and to copy the words, and He told us their true meaning. I have guarded them with my very life to this day and have taught them fervently to my children."

Baqash looked at the tablets with great interest, wondering what story they might tell of how all things came into being. He wanted to hear what the tablets had to say, for they might hold for him the answers to many questions he had had all his life. Doubt crept into his mind because this was all so new and so foreign to what he had heard. He determined, though, that because of what he had seen in these people, there had to be something to the tablets that caused them to live or die for what they said.

"Do you sincerely want to know the truth, my son?" the old man queried.

Baqash was irritated by this question, for it brought to mind all that he had been through to come to this place. But then it hit him that this was a question he must honestly answer. He suddenly realized that truth does not change, that he would have to be the one to change and to learn what had been untrue all his life. He would have to adjust to the truth because the truth would never adjust to him. To learn the truth he would have to be willing to receive it for what it is, not what he wanted it to be. With these thoughts in his heart and mind, Baqash replied, "Yes, Old and Wise One, I want to know the truth."

"Then I will read the truth to you, my son, written by the very finger of your Creator," said Adam, the Old and Wise One. He took the first tablet and began to read it as though he had it memorized.

"In the beginning moment of time, Elohim created all of space and filled it with the elements of all material things. And the elements were without structure and usability. The Spirit of Elohim then gave energy to the elements, and a sphere of water came into being, but it was in total darkness. And Elohim said, 'Let My light be in the creation,' and His light was. And Elohim separated His light from the darkness, and He called His light good, and there was evening and morning, the first day."

The old man continued to read about a second day in which Elohim formed an invisible water vapor covering around the earth. Then on the third day, He formed the dry land out of the water and brought forth all kinds of vegetation to cover the earth. Baqash was confused to hear that the sun, moon, and stars were created on the fourth day, after the earth had already been in existence. He had always thought that the universe and stars were in existence before the earth as the host of Lucifer's legions. It did not surprise him, though, that they were created for times and for seasons because he had learned as a young boy how to read the rotations and revolutions of the earth according to the sun, moon, and stars in their constellations.

The old man read on from the tablet in a raspy, whispering voice. He read about the fifth day and the creation of sea life, including the mighty sea dragon, leviathan, one animal Baqash did not wish to encounter again. Adam told of the creation of the birds that now filled the skies, and Baqash noticed that the story made it clear that all the plants, sea animals, and birds had been created according to their own kinds. They had not developed from lesser kinds to more advanced kinds; they were all created separate and distinct from one another.

Another point that became more and more glaringly evident

to Baqash was that the writings recorded that Elohim did all of His creating with His spoken word. He had the power to call all things into existence from nothing. If this was true, then Elohim had to be truth Himself, for all things exist because he pre-existed all things and brought them into physical existence. Could it be that Lucifer and his angels came from Elohim as well?

Adam gently laid down the first tablet and then picked up the second. This tablet told of the sixth day, in which all the land animals from insects to the mighty beasts like Koah, the behemoth, and the even larger, long-necked giants who could eat from the tops of trees while standing on the ground, wagging their tree-sized tails behind them.

The story finally came to the creation of man. Baqash was caught by surprise when it told of how man and woman together were created in the very likeness of Elohim Himself. The tablet also told how God gave the man and woman dominion over all He had made and that all was to be under his power and authority. *If that is true,* he thought, *then how did Lucifer get control of everything?*

As the sixth day was ended, the account reaffirmed something that had earlier brought questions to Baqash's mind. The tablets kept saying that what Elohim made was good. And now, at the end, the story repeated, even more strongly, that all that Elohim had made was very good. *How could all the pain and suffering in the world be good?* Baqash mused. *How could there be such things as hate, greed, murder, and war if all is very good? This God Elohim has a warped sense of what is good if He thinks the world He created is good.*

The story finished with an account of the seventh day, which was called a day of Sabbath rest. It made it clear that Elohim was no longer doing any creative work in this known universe. It was the final day of the creation week, and at its end began the seven-day cycle of weeks that made the revolutions around the sun work most precisely with the twelve cycles of the full moon. The creation account was certainly consistent with what the stars had taught him about the earth's movement in space related to the sun, moon, and stars. The final words of the second tablet said, "This is the account of the heavens and the earth when they were created in the day that Elohim made earth and heaven."

After he finished reading the tablets, Adam carefully wrapped them in their protective blankets and laid them back in the gold box. He looked at Baqash and said, "I am the man the tablet speaks of. My wife, whom I named Eve because she became the mother of all the living, died in childbirth with our thirtieth child. All of humanity has descended from our seed. Most have gone the way of Lucifer, the father of lies, and deserted the truth; some have been killed for loving the truth." He paused a moment as tears reddened his eyes. Regaining his composure, he spoke again. "I am the responsible one. I chose to distrust the word of Elohim because of the deception of that serpent, who was filled with Lucifer. When I did, the goodness of the presence of Elohim left me and my wife, Eve. Now each of our seed has come into the world dead to the presence of the goodness of Elohim within them."

Baqash did not know what to say. He was awestruck by the possibility of being seated at the feet of the first man created into existence. Questions raced through his mind, yet he did not know how to ask them. He wanted to hear this very unusual old man's story, but he was hesitant to ask because he did not want Adam to think he was questioning the message of the tablets, at least for now. Baqash felt he needed more information before he could truly know what to believe about all that he was hearing.

There was a reason they referred to this man named Adam as the Old and Wise One: he could oftentimes discern what was in the mind of a man before being told. His many years of living had given him the ability to feel what others were feeling.

"I can tell you do not know what to believe about all this. It is not surprising, knowing what you have been taught since you were a child—all the many lies about the so-called serpent god, Lucifer, who is nothing but a fallen, rebellious angel whom Elohim has seen fit to use as a tool to test the hearts of fallen men."

The words *fallen men* gave Baqash something to grasp as a means to finally break his silence. "What do you mean by 'fallen men'?" he asked.

"Because you hunger to know, I will tell you what I mean by telling you how I fell and thus caused your own fallenness in your relationships with our Creator Elohim." The wise old man leaned forward on the cushions on which he sat, as though he intended to speak more directly than he already had to this seeker of the truth.

"The first thing I remember seeing, as my body filled with life and I opened my eyes, was a face filled with brilliant light and a broad, approving smile. The light was bright, but my eyes were not offended by its brightness. The smile was an expression of the purest love that I would only learn to appreciate much later, when it was too late. As this wonderful spirit person took my hand and raised me to my feet, I was enveloped with total goodness within and perfect peace that I took completely for granted until it left me to myself."

"As I have already said, my wife was formed from a piece of my side so that we would understand that we were created by our Maker to be in oneness with each other, just as Elohim was at one with Himself and desired that we be one with Him in love and peace. Elohim placed us in a beautiful garden He had planted and called Eden, the very same garden you seek. My wife and I lived in Eden in complete harmony with each other and with Elohim. He came to enjoy companionship and fellowship with us every day, and He taught us the meaning of the tablets and to read and write with the same words He Himself had written. He also taught us to read the sun, moon, and stars to know the seasons. What all men know today came from what we learned from Elohim. He taught us about the plants in the garden and how we could care for them in the most perfect way, and we learned about the animals and the purpose for which each was created. All of these things we would pass on to the children whom Elohim would give to us in time.

"Elohim made it clear to us that He wanted us to love Him in freedom, out of a trust we had, that His word was true. He also told us that in order for this kind of relationship to be possible, He had to give us a choice to trust and obey His word. He said that if we chose not to trust Him, we would be held responsible for our choice. He took us into the center of the garden where He had created two different trees. One was what He called the Tree of Life.

He said that as long as we ate from it, we would live forever in His presence. We learned later that this was not a magic tree. The true power of the tree was our trust in Elohim's word. It was Elohim Himself who gave us our lives.

"The second tree he called the Tree of the Knowledge of Good and Evil. He told us that if we ever questioned His word and ate of this tree, we would surely be responsible to him for our rebellion, and the consequence would be death. At that time we had no idea what He meant by this thing called death, for it was something we had never seen before. All we had seen was life everywhere around us, and all was filled with nothing but goodness.

"We lived in the garden in total goodness and love for one hundred revolutions, but we were not prepared for the test Elohim would allow us to endure. We did not know that Lucifer had rebelled against Elohim, desiring to make himself equal with Lord Elohim. His strategy was, by deceiving us into distrusting Elohim, to take the dominion over the earth that Elohim had given to me and my wife. He would trick us into eating of the forbidden tree. Elohim allowed this test of our trust so that we could establish our love and obedience to Him alone. I have learned that true love and goodness are best expressed when they are tried for their sincerity.

"My most beautiful Eve and I failed the test miserably. We had become very familiar with Elohim and were taking Him entirely for granted. We did not know how vulnerable we were to this kind of temptation. Lucifer came to us, using as a cover for his deception the most appealing animal in the garden at that time. He spoke through the serpent in a way we had never even conceived of before. He put questions into our minds that we had never thought possible, questions that planted seeds of doubt about Elohim's honesty. But then there was the most tempting of all thoughts: the possibility of becoming equal to Elohim Himself. As I pondered these new thoughts, Eve had already been convinced to eat the forbidden fruit. I had not thought things through to their obvious conclusion, and I had not previously made a firm commitment to resist this kind of temptation. So when Eve presented to me some of the fruit from the Tree of the Knowledge of Good and Evil, I saw its allure, and I saw the possibility of being as great as Elohim, and I ate of it as well.

"It was then that we both learned the knowledge of good and evil and the meaning of death. The love and goodness that was a part of our very being left us both the moment I made our joint rebellion complete. We came to understand that the goodness and love we had had was the very presence of Elohim within us, and when we chose to distrust His word, His presence was removed from us. We became just like Lucifer: created beings left to ourselves away from Elohim's presence. We came to know what good was by no longer possessing it. Elohim had removed His presence from us, and our ability to relate to Him died, for we died in our spirits, which was the goodness of Elohim Himself in us. We then knew that evil was the absence of the presence of the good of Elohim. We still knew what good was, but we could no longer produce it from within ourselves. We were fallen from living good to living evil.

"In this new fallen state of being, Elohim forced us from the garden so we would no longer have access to the Tree of Life. He placed a guardian angel in the garden to keep us and our descendants from ever entering it again. And because we chose to trust Lucifer rather than Elohim, from that day forward Lucifer has had dominion over the earth and all of mankind. But Elohim in His goodness and love has given us a promise that if we trust His word once again, He will one day raise up someone to deliver us from Lucifer's rule and our bondage to our own lack of good within us. This deliverer will come from the seed of woman. Elohim now fights against Lucifer for those who put their faith and trust in this promised deliverer."

Baqash sat speechless before the withered old man, his head bowed in contemplation. He wanted to believe this story so badly because he wanted what he had seen in Adoniel, Megado, Shadi, and now Adam, but to believe it meant he would never be the same self-sufficient man again. To believe, he would have to exchange his all-consuming hate for Lucifer for belief in a newfound Creator whom he knew so little of. But there was a knowledge within himself that confirmed that what he had heard was the truth and his only hope.

The broken but now convinced young seeker knew deep inside himself that he had no choice but to believe in Elohim. He looked into the eyes of Adam and then bowed before his newfound forefather, crying out with the liberated tears of a new faith, "O my father, I believe!"

Though it took every ounce of strength he had, the old man slowly rose from where he was seated and shuffled over to Baqash, whose face was bowed low to the ground. Adam knelt beside his restored child and wept with him. The men of the Line of Light stood and gathered around the pair, quietly singing a song of praise to Elohim.

Twenty-One

Eden's Veil

During the next few rotations Baqash was allowed to visit the Old and Wise One periodically. The old man's strength had begun to fail during the last revolution, and he did not have much more time to live on the earth. Adam answered many of Baqash's questions, which helped him understand why things were as they had become. Adam had Lamech read Baqash the account he had written of his experience on his creation day, his account of the temptation and fall, and the story of his first two sons, Cain and Abel.

This story of the man named Cain who killed his younger brother was of great interest to Baqash because his father had told him tales about a distant forefather named Cain who had a son named La-mech. This man Cain, who lived in the land of Nod, was the reason that many of the men in his family had been given a similar name. So many things in Baqash's way of thinking were beginning to fit together like a wagon's missing parts that had been found to make it possible to repair. Baqash's understanding of the truth was being transformed more and more with each new rotation. Life was beginning to make sense, and his awareness of Elohim was deepening with each illumination.

There was something, though, that Baqash felt he still had to do. He had come all this way, thinking that he needed to see this Garden of Eden, this place of delight Adoniel had told him about, and he felt compelled to see it with his new understanding. Shadi had told him it would not be all that he thought it would be, but Baqash was convinced that he needed to see it anyway.

He finally persuaded Shadi to ride with him and show him where to find the garden. He told Shadi that he would go looking for it even if he didn't accompany him, so his friend and newfound brother in Elohim agreed to go. They left one morning in the early light of dawn. The garden was a two-rotation ride further up the river that flowed from Eden, so they mounted their megalosaurs and headed north with their guardian, Koah, following close behind.

They came out of the hills by midday and began to cross a vast, fertile crescent of flat grazing land. Herds of beasts grazed everywhere: large woolly mammoths, giant rhinoceroses, all kinds of cattle, deer, and grass-eating dinosaurs. They also saw lions, tigers, and wild dogs. All thrived on the lush grasses and berry bushes that abounded there. Often Koah stopped and frolicked with some of the animals he encountered; then he ran to catch up with his fellow travelers as they proceeded at a leisurely trotting pace.

The two men had much to talk about as they rode along together. Shadi told how his parents already wanted to make arrangements for his marriage to one of the young women of the clan. They had mentioned several possibilities to him, but none had yet struck his fancy.

Baqash, on the other hand, talked about making a return trip to his own family. He knew it would be a dangerous trip, but he felt he must tell them what he had found in the truth of Elohim. He also knew he would not leave until he felt he was strong enough in his faith to face the struggles of a hostile world, including many in his own household. He hoped that Landua would be open to receive the message he would bring because he knew that they would never have a life together if she could not be one with him in his love for Elohim. He began to pray to Elohim that He would help her to see what he could see in his heart.

On the second day of travel, the pair approached what looked like a deep, dark forest, which disturbed Baqash. According to what Shadi had said, the garden should be very near, but from the looks of this deeply wooded, thorn- and thistle-laden forest, it had to be rotations beyond here. Suddenly Shadi pulled his megalosaur to a halt and commanded, "We must stop here. We should go no further."

"Why?" asked Baqash, sensing that Shadi knew of some danger that he could not see.

"Remember the Old and Wise One has said that Elohim stationed an angel to keep men out of the garden and away from the Tree of Life?" said Shadi.

"Yes, I know. But we have not come to the beautiful garden yet," said Baqash impatiently.

"That is the garden," said Shadi solemnly, gesturing toward the forest of thorns and thistles. "After Elohim forced our first parents from Eden and cursed the ground with thorns and thistles, there was no one to care for it anymore. It is now veiled as a result of our rebellion and is nothing more than a reminder of what we have become compared to what we used to be. The fruit trees have long since been choked out by the weeds, and the former beauty has changed into a thick, dark place of death. The Tree of Life is still in the midst of the garden, but no one could get to it now—even if there was no angel to keep him away. The consequences of the curse on the ground are more evident here than any place on earth.

Baqash looked at the garden of weeds. It spread for miles in front of him, as far as he could see in both directions. He could not believe that what had once been a place called "delight" had become a place that could only be called desolate. He determined that he would ride just a little closer to get a better look at what he had come so far to see. Despite Shadi's cries of warning and calls to come back, he rode off toward the twisted mass of dead vines, rotted trees, large weeds, and thorny briars. The closer he got, the uglier the garden became.

As he galloped toward the patch of briars, looking intently at the tangled, thorn-ridden corruption of beauty, from out of nowhere a flash of light came from far above. The flash was a pendulum of brightness that swished down across his path. The megalosaur fell to its knees and lurched to the side, trying to avoid the swath of silvery light. Baqash was thrown side away from his saddle, rolling several times from the force of his fall. As he turned onto his back and looked up to see what had caused the flash of flaming, silver light, he saw the figure of a human-like being, clothed in a robe as white as purest light. The figure stood so tall that his form would have dwarfed the largest of the Violent Ones, and his grandeur far outshone anything Baqash had ever seen. His eyes glared more fiercely than the leviathan's. Even that powerful creature could not withstand the power of this mighty angel of Elohim.

Baqash rolled to his hands and knees and crawled as quickly as he could to try to avoid the flaming sword the angel was wielding. He finally got to his feet and ran fearfully back toward Shadi. His megalosaur passed him at full speed, squealing with terror. Shadi took off after it as Baqash continued to distance himself as fast as he could from the giant angel. He had been a warrior all his life and had learned to control his fear, but for the first time he was as terror-stricken as his megalosaur.

Baqash sensed that he was not being chased, so he slowed to a fast walk and turned to glance back as he continued to move away from the garden. To his great relief, the angel was no longer there. The twisted, gnarled expanse of thorny weeds was all that could be seen in the distance.

Now Baqash stopped and turned back to look fully toward the garden once again. There was no doubt in his mind about the angel with the flaming sword that the Old and Wise One had said guarded Eden. Although the garden was not what he had thought it would be, he knew that the testimony of the first man, Adam, was true. The angelic sentry was certainly a confirmation of that, but Baqash realized that he had already come to believe in Eden before this supernatural confirmation had come. He knew this to be true, for when he had left he shepherd camp with Shadi, his reason for the journey was no longer to see something he hoped would be there. Instead he had traveled to see a garden he was already convinced was there. His hair-raising experience had only confirmed what he already believed was true.

Just then Shadi arrived after chasing down Baqash's megalosaur. "Are you all right?" he asked, handing the reins to his friend. "What did you see over there that gave this animal such a scare? It is still trembling and is as jumpy as a freshly shorn sheep."

"The angel that our forefather spoke of is truly there. I saw him with my own eyes and still tremble as much as this poor animal. You were right to give me warning. I surely did not know what I was headed toward, but now that I have survived this encounter, I have truly grown much in my faith. I have seen with my eyes what I already believed with my heart. I will never be the same again." Baqash paused for few minutes to collect himself and allow his animal to calm down. He then mounted and said, "I have seen all I needed to see. Now I can get on with my life. Let's go home."

The two men turned south and headed down the river that flowed from Eden. Their companion, Koah, followed along behind, stopping occasionally to sniff the flowers in the grass and then eat them.

It was evening in the camp when they rode in a few rotations later. They took care of the animals and then returned to the people of Elohim, who were beginning the Sabbath sacrifice. Seth, now the oldest of the Line of Light still able to do so, slew the lamb without blemish, allowing the blood to drain on the ground. He laid the animal on the altar of uncut stacked stones and then burned the lamb with fire. As the smoke from the sacrifice rose into the sky, Baqash remembered something that the Old and Wise One had said. "Now that death has come, forgiveness can only be given through the shed blood of the lamb, for the life is in the blood." Baqash bowed his head and thanked Elohim for the lamb that was slain. He then thanked Him that the veil of lies had been removed from his heart so he could know the truth. Baqash could now see with his heart what his slave, Megado, had come to believe long before him. He knew now that he was finally a truly free man. The seeker had been found by the One he had been searching for.